Pytorch Deep Learning by Example, Vol.2 (3rd Edition)

Contents

List of Figures

List of Tables

Do you have difficulties to even get started on pytorch?
Do you have trouble to really understand pytorch example
code?
Do you want to understand many state-of-art deep
learning technologies with bare-minimum math?
Do you have obstacles to implement a real life deep
learning projects in pytorch?

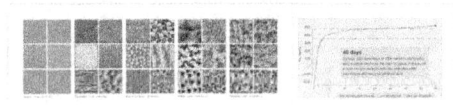

This book series will easy these pains and help you learn and grasp deep learning technology
from ground zero with m
any interesting real world examples implemented in pytorch.

In this book series, you will learn:

* a basic deep learning concepts/theory with bare-minimum math
* a deep-dived/well-explained MNIST CNN example so that you can really understand pytorch
model, how to choose loss,
optimizer in pytorch etc.
* how to use a pre-trained model by using transfer learning/fine-tune techniques.
* what are CNN, RNN, Seq2Seq,word embedding, CTC, Auto-encoder, DMN,
DQN/DDQN,MCTS,Alphago/Alphazero etc, and how the
y work.
* How those deep learning technologies are applied to NLP, OCR, Speech, Computer Games etc.

This is Volume 2.

Benjamin Young

Pytorch Deep Learning by Example Vol. 2

Applications - Grasp deep Learning from
scratch like AlphaGo Zero within 40 days [3rd
Edition]

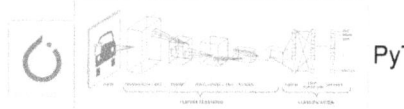

PyTorch

Benjamin Young

Copyright

For permission requests, email to author, at the address below:

benjamin@comrite.com

Web URL: http://www.comrite.com

Preface

Artificial Intelligence (AI) could be traced back to the 1950s. It went through several hype/bust cycles. In 2010, we entered the era of AI, this time deep learning (a branch of AI) took a leading role.

Over the past years, deep learning has gone from a niche field comprised of a few researchers to being sort of mainstream. It made incredibly progress in many areas, such as: image classification, voice recognition, text generation, language translation etc.

As time goes by, it became apparent that deep learning would stay in the mainstream.

As a technology person, it is time to keep updated with these new skill sets.

Well, to really understand deep learning, a deep dive into math is normally needed.

Fortunately, tech world/knowledge are normally built on layers/blocks. Researchers/scientists have built a great deep learning foundation for us, we will stand on the shoulders of giants. In this book we will mainly focus on applications on top of them. From practical engineering point of view, We may not need a deep dive into math in order to use it effectively. Just like we can write an awesome software running on CPU, we generally do not need to have a very deep understanding of CPU.

So in this book, we are not trying to deep dive into the math, instead we are trying to get an intuition of neural network, understand deep learning deep enough so that we could use and apply it effectively in our daily job/use cases.

I hope this book could help others who do not have a formal deep learning/AI course/training to learn deep learning quickly.

Example source code could be found at:

https://github.com/mingewang/pytorch_deep_learning_by_example

Remember, being a relatively new technology, deep learning is not perfect. It requires an investment of both time and money, as well as the expertise to use it, not just for the researcher, but for the programmer too.

I welcome emails from any readers with comments, suggestions, or bug fixes.

Benjamin Young

benjamin@comrite.com

Aug, 2019

About Volume I/II

Volume I is focused on deep learning, and pytorch fundamentals.

Volume II is focused on advanced applications.

Disclaimer

Although the author and publisher have made every effort to ensure that the information in this book was correct at press time, the author and publisher do not assume and hereby disclaim any liability to any party for any loss, damage, or disruption caused by errors or omissions, whether such errors or omissions result from negligence, accident, or any other cause.

Acknowledgments

I would like to thank the invaluable support from my family for their patience while I worked late, often and sometimes on vacation.

Chapter 1

Natural Language Processing

Natural Language Processing (NLP) is about how to program computers to process and analyze large amounts of natural language data.

With the advance of machine learning, deep learning, NLP is shifting from statistical methods to neural network methods.

Many applications can be categorized as NLP problems, For example:

- Text Classification: DNN is good at those kinds of tasks. One typical application is email spam filtering.

- Sentiment Analysis: To determine, from a text corpus, whether the sentiment towards any topic or product etc. is positive, negative, or neutral.

- Language Modeling: the name sounds quite academic, but the main task is to predict the next word given the previous words. As we showed in the previous chapter, an RNN can learn the probabilistic structure from the training data, then generate a new sequence of data which are statistically consistent with the source data.

- Speech Recognition: to generate human-understandable words/text based on speech/audio data. We will see how DNN be applied in this area in a later chapter in this book.

- Caption Generation: for example, given a digital image, such as a photo, generate a textual description of the contents of the image. Actually, we use CNN + RNN to achieve this.

- Language/Machine Translation: to automatically translate a text or speech from one language to another, it is one of the most important applications of NLP. We see how a DNN could be applied in this chapter.

- Document Summarization: to generate a short description of a text document.

- Question AnsweringFAQ, to generate an answer based on a document. We will see this in this chapter.

...

Actually, NLP is a very broad area, it involves many areas: speech recognition, natural language understanding, and natural language generation etc.

In this chapter, we will focus mainly on language translation, text processing. We will see how we can apply The neural network, deep learning to this area.

1.1 text processing and NLP packages

A common task in many ML applications involves **text processing** or **text analysis**.

Traditionally, text processing may refer to:

- search and replace (e.g.: using a regular expression)

- format

- generate a processed report of the content of, or

- filter a file or report of a text file.

- a tokenizer to vectorize a text corpus, by turning each text into either a sequence of integers (each integer is the index of a token in a dictionary) or into a vector where the coefficient for each token could be binary, based on word count, etc.

- text_to_word_sequence to convert a text to a sequence of words etc

...

There are several python NLP libs/packages address those issues:

- **Torchtext** is a package, consists of data processing utilities and popular datasets for natural language. It provides a set of data-abstractions that helps read and process raw text data into PyTorch tensors. It can load the data in whatever format your deep learning framework requires.

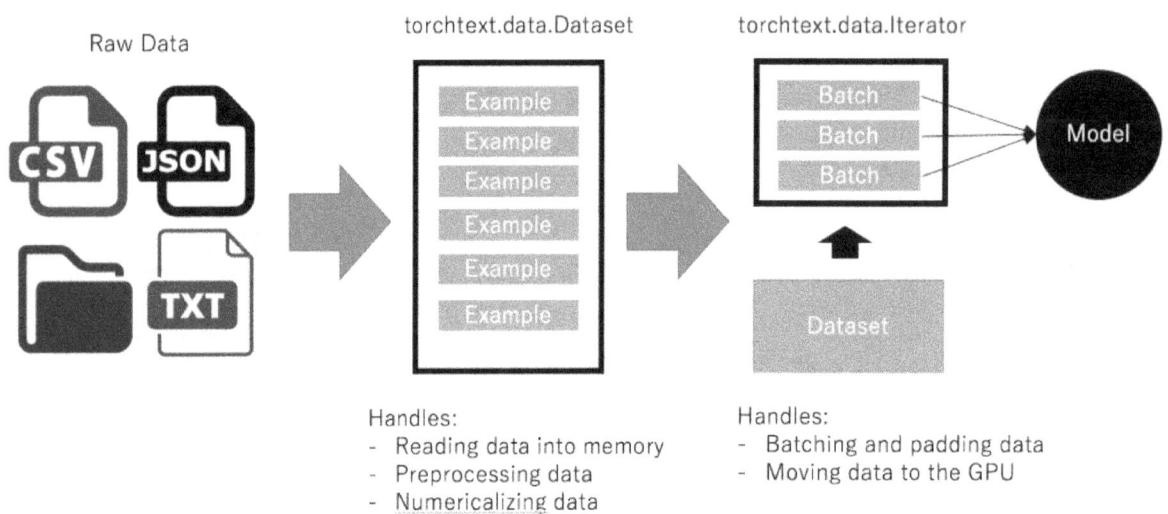

Figure 1.1: torchtext import raw data as pytorch dataset

You can find more documents at:
https://pytext-pytext.readthedocs-hosted.com/en/latest/index.html

- **PyTorch-NLP** is a library for Natural Language Processing (NLP) in Python. It's built with the very latest research in mind, and was designed from day one to support rapid prototyping. PyTorch-NLP comes with pre-trained embeddings, samplers, dataset loaders, metrics, neural network modules, and text encoders, etc.
  Torchtext and PyTorch-NLP differ in the architecture and feature set; otherwise, they are similar.
  You can find more at:
  https://github.com/PetrochukM/PyTorch-NLP
  https://pytorchnlp.readthedocs.io/en/latest/

- **PyText** is a deep-learning-based NLP modeling framework built on PyTorch, it is a new framework released in Dec, 2018 by facebook.
  Internally (at the time of writing), PyText uses torchtext for training-time data reading and pre-processing. However, it's very new.
  More document can be found at:

https://pytext-pytext.readthedocs-hosted.com/en/latest/
https://github.com/facebookresearch/pytext

- **AllenNLP** is a great NLP modeling library that is aimed at providing reference implementations and pre-built state-of-the-art models, and make it easy to iterate on and research with models for different NLP tasks. Currently, it is not yet mature, not optimized for speed.
  More document can be found at:
  https://allenai.github.io/allennlp-docs/

- **spaCy** is a mature and batteries-included framework that comes with prebuilt models for common NLP tasks like classification, named entity recognition, and part-of-speech tagging, etc. It is easy to use, very fast, ready for production, but not easy to do customization etc.
  More document can be found at:
  https://spacy.io/

As you can image, each package has its own pros and cons, and is evolving rapidly. I, personally, can not tell which one is better at the time of writing. Readers can read more documents to find which one suits their needs best.

Tip
Pytorch has some good tutorials at: https://pytorch.org/tutorials/beginner/deep_learning_nlp_tutorial.html

---

1.2   Word embedding

An NLP application usually involves a language made of words. So how we handle words is quite critical.

In this section, we will talk about an important technique in NLP called **word embedding**.

1.2.1   Word embedding concept

Remember, in some previous text related examples, we used one-hot encoded vector to represent a word/token, which is then fed into a neural network for training. As you can imagine, each vector is quite sparse as inside it, most bits are zeros. If the vocabulary is large, this means we need a high-dimensional matrix/tensor to represent an input. That means a waste of computing resources.

People came up with a technique called **word vector** or **word embedding** to mitigate this problem. The main idea is to compact several words/tokens into one vector. Thus, we will get a **dense, low-dimensional representation** of our vocabulary. Ideally, we want similar words to have similar representations. For example, the representation of "red", "yellow" could be similar compared to "car".

Quote from Wikipedia:

```
1  Word embedding is the collective name for a set of language modeling
2  and feature learning techniques in natural language processing (NLP)
3  where words or phrases from the vocabulary are mapped to vectors
4  of real numbers. Conceptually it involves a mathematical embedding
5  from a space with one dimension per word
6  to a continuous vector space with a much lower dimension.
```

Roughly speaking, word embedding generally tries to map a word to a dense vector (instead of a sparse vector) using a dictionary.

For example, we can use an integer i (e.g: 4) to represent a specific word, e.g: hello, then we map 4 as a dense vector [0.25, 0.1], and keep this mapping using a dictionary:

dict[4] = word_vector ([0.25, 0.1])

1.2.2   pytroch embedding layer

Pytorch provides an **embedding layer** to do this mapping for us. Also the embedding layer can be trained by the network to suite our specific needs.

According to pytorch document:
https://pytorch.org/docs/stable/nn.html#sparse-layers

```
1   torch.nn.Embedding(num_embeddings, embedding_dim, padding_idx=None, max_norm=None ↩
        ,
2   norm_type=2.0, scale_grad_by_freq=False, sparse=False, _weight=None)
3
4   A simple lookup table that stores embeddings of a fixed dictionary and size.
5
6   This module is often used to store word embeddings and
7   retrieve them using indices.
8
9   The input to the module is a list of indices,
10  and the output is the corresponding word embeddings.
```

```
11
12  Parameters:
13
14  num_embeddings (int) - size of the dictionary of embeddings
15
16  embedding_dim (int) - the size of each embedding vector
17
18  Other parameters are optional.
```

Let's look at a simple example to understand it. Imagining our training set consists only of two phrases:

- Hope to see you soon

- Nice to see you again

First, we encode these phrases by assigning each word a unique integer number, then our phrases could be rewritten as:

```
1  [0, 1, 2, 3, 4]
2  [5, 1, 2, 3, 6]
```

We can feed this data into an embedding layer like this:

```
1  ...
2  embedding = torch.nn.Embedding(7, 2))
3  embedding(input)
4  ...
```

The first argument 7 is the **number of distinct words** in the training set. The second argument 2 indicates the **size of the embedding vectors**.

You may ask how come a 2-dimensional vector can represent the 7 tokens? Well, pytorch uses two floating-point numbers in that vector. Two floating points or even one floating could represent the infinite number of words. That is how we can encode many tokens into a dense vector.

Once the network has been trained, the embedding layer can be thought of as having some internal table. In this case, it will be a table of size (7, 2) as following which are used to map integers to embedding vectors: (the number for just imaginary for now)

```
1  +------------+------------+
2  |   index    |  Embedding |
3  +------------+------------+
4  |     0      | [1.2, 3.1] |
5  |     1      | [0.1, 4.2] |
6  |     2      | [1.0, 3.1] |
7  |     3      | [0.3, 2.1] |
8  |     4      | [2.2, 1.4] |
9  |     5      | [0.7, 1.7] |
10 |     6      | [4.1, 2.0] |
11 +------------+------------+
```

Thus, according to these embeddings, our second training phrase will be represented as:

```
1  [[0.7, 1.7], [0.1, 4.2], [1.0, 3.1], [0.3, 2.1], [4.1, 2.0]]
```

As we said earlier, the output of an embedding layer is, normally, fed to an RNN or 1D convolution layer or other layers, thus the embedding layer and other layers will be trained together by that data.

Once trained, the embedding space will show a lot of structure, which are specifically trained for the problem we are trying to solve.

The following figure showed some good examples:

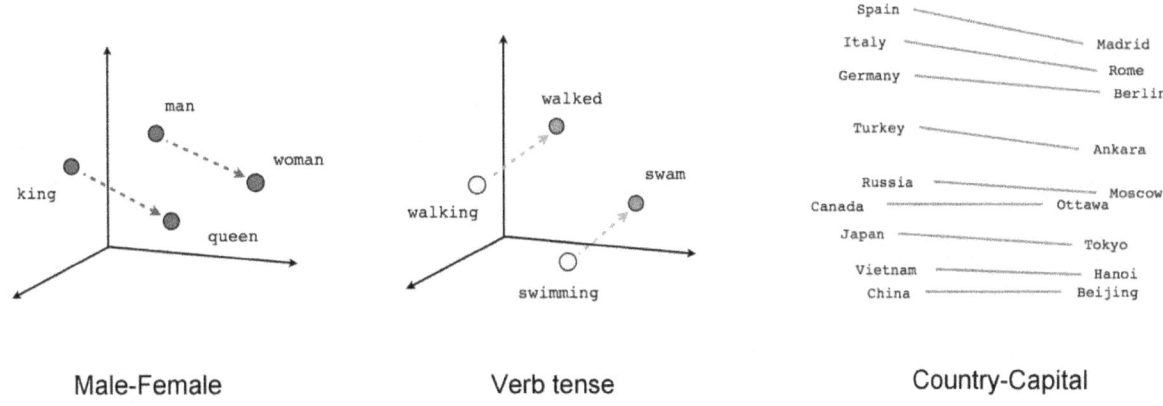

Figure 1.2: word embedding structure after training

We will see another detailed example in the next section shortly, so that you will understand better how the embedding layer is trained.

1.2.3   an example of training word embedding layer

This example will show you how an embedding layer be trained combining with other layers.

In this example, we will label our words/documents first, then we plot words in an embedding space. That plot will show a specific structures for this specific problem!

Here is the code:

```
1  # pytorch sample to show word embedding
2  import torch
3  import torch.nn as nn
4  import torch.nn.functional as F
5  import torch.optim as optim
6  import torchvision
7
8  from numpy import array
9  from torchnlp.text_encoders import WhitespaceEncoder
```

```
10  from torchnlp.utils import pad_tensor
11  import matplotlib.pyplot as plt
12
13  # doc/words and its label
14  docs = ['China',
15      'Italy',
16      'Germany',
17      'USA',
18      'Canada',
19      'Beijing',
20      'Rome',
21      'Berlin',
22      'Washington DC',
23      'Ottawa']
24
25  # define class labels
26  labels = array([1,1,1,1,1,0,0,0,0,0])
27
28
29  # we use integer to encode/represent the documents's word
30  # here we use torchnlp's Tokenizer
31  t  = WhitespaceEncoder( docs )
32  # t.vocab
33
34  # encode the whole document
35  encoded_docs =[ t.encode(x) for x in docs]
36  print("encoded_docs is:")
37  print(encoded_docs)
38  # encoded_docs will look this
39  #[tensor([5]),
40  # tensor([6]),
41  # tensor([7]),
42  ## tensor([8]),
43  # tensor([9]),
44  # tensor([10]),
45  # tensor([11]),
46  # tensor([12]),
47  # tensor([13, 14]),
48  # tensor([15])
49
50  # Each doc/sequences could have different lengths
51  # and pytorch prefers
```

```python
52    # all inputs to have the same length.
53    # here we will pad all input sequences to have the length of 2
54    max_length = 2
55    padded_docs = [ pad_tensor(x, max_length) for x in encoded_docs ]
56    print("padded_docs is:")
57    print(padded_docs)
58
59    # now define our DNN module:
60    # we use nn.Embedding, then a linear layer with sigmoid
61    # for our binary classification
62    class MyNet(torch.nn.Module):
63      # num_embeddings : vocab_size
64      # embedding_dim:  the size of each embedding vector
65      # max_length: the input max length
66      # n_out: final out, here we set 1
67      # as we will use sigmoid for our binary classification
68      def __init__(self, num_embeddings, embedding_dim, max_length, n_out):
69        super(MyNet, self).__init__()
70    # nn.embedding layers
71    # first parameter: size of the vocabulary
72    # second parameter: output_dim, Dimension of the dense embedding.
73    # We will choose a small embedding space of 2 dimensions for easy plotting
74        self.em = torch.nn.Embedding(num_embeddings, embedding_dim)
75        # n_out is 1 here for binary classification
76        self.linear_1 = torch.nn.Linear( max_length * embedding_dim, n_out)
77
78      def forward(self, x):
79        y = self.em(x)
80        # need to flatten/squeeze, but keep the first dimension ( batch ) the same
81        y = y.view(y.size()[0], -1)
82        y = self.linear_1(y)
83        y= torch.sigmoid(y)
84        return y
85
86      # helper function, embedding encode a token (x) for easy plot
87      def embedding_encode(self, x):
88        return self.em(x)
89
90    # let's create a model
91    num_embeddings = t.vocab_size
92    embedding_dim = 2
93    n_out = 1  # two classes
```

```
94  model = MyNet( num_embeddings, embedding_dim, max_length, n_out)
95
96  # Construct the loss function
97  # for binary classification
98  criterion = nn.BCELoss()
99  # Construct the optimizer,
100 # learning rate (lr) need trial-error
101 # if lr too small, learning will be very slow
102 optimizer = optim.Adam(model.parameters(), lr=0.8 )
103
104 epochs = 5
105 batch_size = 2
106
107 # convert from list of tensor to pure tensor (*,2)
108 # so x_train is: [ [s11,s12], [s21,s22], ...]
109 x_train = torch.stack(padded_docs)
110 # make sure y_train the same as input
111 # so y_train is: [ [y1], [y2], ...]
112 y_train = torch.from_numpy(labels).float().view(-1,1)
113
114 model.train()
115 # training process, calculate Gradient Descent
116 for epoch in range(epochs):
117     i = 0;
118     print('epoch: ', epoch,' begin .. ')
119     # batch feeding the data
120     for i in range(0, x_train.size()[0], batch_size):
121
122         # start debugger
123         #import pdb; pdb.set_trace()
124
125         # get a batch of data
126         x = x_train[i:i+batch_size]
127         y = y_train[i:i+batch_size]
128
129         # Forward pass: Compute predicted y by passing x to the model
130         y_pred = model(x)
131
132         # Compute and print loss
133         loss = criterion(y_pred, y)
134         print('i: ', i,' loss: ', loss.item() )
135
```

```python
        # Zero gradients, perform a backward pass and update the weights.
        optimizer.zero_grad()

        # perform a backward pass (back propagation)
        loss.backward()

        # Update the parameters
        optimizer.step()

# Let's try to plot the what is the embedding
labels = []
data_x = []
data_y = []

model.eval()
# plot all the words we learned
for k in t.vocab:
  # encode using our token ( from string to int)
  encoded_k = t.encode(k)
  labels.append(k)
  # now let's use embedding to encode int to its representation
  tmp = model.embedding_encode(encoded_k)
  x = tmp[0][0].item()
  y = tmp[0][1].item()
  data_x.append( x )
  data_y.append( y )
  print("city is:", k, " encoded as:", encoded_k, " in embedding space, x=", x, " ↩
      , y=",y)

plt.plot(data_x, data_y, 'ro')

# add label to each word point in the (x,y) space
for label, x, y in zip(labels, data_x, data_y):
    plt.annotate(
        label,
        xy=(x, y), xytext=(-20, 20),
        textcoords='offset points', ha='right', va='bottom',
        bbox=dict(boxstyle='round,pad=0.5', fc='yellow', alpha=0.5),
        arrowprops=dict(arrowstyle = '->', connectionstyle='arc3,rad=0'))

plt.show()
```

Tip

You can download the complete code of this example from the author's repo
(https://github.com/mingewang/pytorch_deep_learning_by_example) at:
nlp/capital_city_token.py

There are many detailed comments inside the code, hope you can understand the code without any problem.

In the code, I used some text process utilities from torchnlp. You can install it easily by using: pip install torchnlp.

- Line 31, the WhitespaceEncoder will encode docs by splitting on whitespace. It basically finds all the unique words and maps them into integers.

- Line 35, we use WhitespaceEncoder.encode to convert the docs (strings) into that integer representations.

- Line 55, we pad those tensors into the same length tensor.

- Line 62 - 88, we define a simple DNN module: an embedding layer and linear layer with sigmoid for **binary classification**. Later, we use pytorch BCELoss(). It is a quite standard way to handle binary classification problems.

Tip

more about cross-entropy loss can be found at: https://gombru.github.io/2018/05/23/cross_entropy_loss/

- Line 89 - 143, are very standard pytorch training codes. The only catch is how to specify the learning rate in Line 102. If too small, it will take lots of time to train.

- Line 150 - 175, we loop all the words, use embedding layer to encode them, then plot it out.

If you run this example, the output should look like following:

```
(pytorch-cpu) $ python capital_city_token.py
encoded_docs is:
[tensor([5]), tensor([6]), tensor([7]), tensor([8]), tensor([9]), tensor([10]),
 tensor([11]), tensor([12]), tensor([13, 14]), tensor([15])]
padded_docs is:
[tensor([5, 0]), tensor([6, 0]), tensor([7, 0]), tensor([8, 0]), tensor([9, 0]),
```

```
7   tensor([10,  0]), tensor([11,  0]), tensor([12,  0]), tensor([13, 14]), tensor ↩
        ([15,  0])]
8   epoch:  0  begin ..
9   i:  0  loss:  0.7931680083274841
10  i:  2  loss:  0.11117324978113174
11  i:  4  loss:  1.3176015615463257
12  i:  6  loss:  1.297735333442688
13  i:  8  loss:  0.10404209792613983
14  epoch:  1  begin ..
15  i:  0  loss:  2.332980155944824
16  i:  2  loss:  0.00023663061438128352
17  i:  4  loss:  5.960465188081798e-08
18  i:  6  loss:  0.0
19  i:  8  loss:  0.0
20  epoch:  2  begin ..
21  i:  0  loss:  1.1920930376163597e-07
22  i:  2  loss:  0.0
23  i:  4  loss:  0.0
24  i:  6  loss:  0.0
25  i:  8  loss:  0.0
26  epoch:  3  begin ..
27  i:  0  loss:  0.0
28  i:  2  loss:  0.0
29  i:  4  loss:  0.0
30  i:  6  loss:  0.0
31  i:  8  loss:  0.0
32  epoch:  4  begin ..
33  i:  0  loss:  0.0
34  i:  2  loss:  0.0
35  i:  4  loss:  0.0
36  i:  6  loss:  0.0
37  i:  8  loss:  0.0
38  city is: <pad>  encoded as: tensor([0])  in embedding space, x= ↩
        1.5985530614852905 , y= -1.7406797409057617
39  city is: <unk>  encoded as: tensor([1])  in embedding space, x= ↩
        1.5590152740478516 , y= -0.9072751998901367
40  city is: </s>  encoded as: tensor([2])  in embedding space, x= ↩
        -0.6343875527381897 , y= 0.8509272336959839
41  city is: <s>  encoded as: tensor([3])  in embedding space, x= 1.700877070426941 , ↩
        y= 0.9995605945587158
42  city is: <copy>  encoded as: tensor([4])  in embedding space, x= ↩
        -0.13159312307834625 , y= 0.046031463891267776
```

```
43  city is: China  encoded as: tensor([5])  in embedding space, x= -6.6091628074646  ↩
      , y= 2.7623276710510254
44  city is: Italy  encoded as: tensor([6])  in embedding space, x=  ↩
      -6.073096752166748 , y= 1.324095368385315
45  city is: Germany  encoded as: tensor([7])  in embedding space, x=  ↩
      -3.9082822799682617 , y= 3.9477412700653076
46  city is: USA  encoded as: tensor([8])  in embedding space, x= -3.037409782409668  ↩
      , y= 4.964270114898682
47  city is: Canada  encoded as: tensor([9])  in embedding space, x=  ↩
      -5.0529866218566895 , y= 4.586971759796143
48  city is: Beijing  encoded as: tensor([10])  in embedding space, x=  ↩
      5.1836981773376465 , y= -4.629574775695801
49  city is: Rome  encoded as: tensor([11])  in embedding space, x=  ↩
      3.6919758319854736 , y= -5.067819118499756
50  city is: Berlin  encoded as: tensor([12])  in embedding space, x=  ↩
      4.141485214233398 , y= -4.114591121673584
51  city is: Washington  encoded as: tensor([13])  in embedding space, x=  ↩
      3.1297452449798584 , y= -3.9657862186431885
52  city is: DC  encoded as: tensor([14])  in embedding space, x= 5.3732829093933105  ↩
      , y= -3.2661495208740234
53  city is: Ottawa  encoded as: tensor([15])  in embedding space, x=  ↩
      4.605438232421875 , y= -3.3444809913635254
```

A figure was plotted as below:

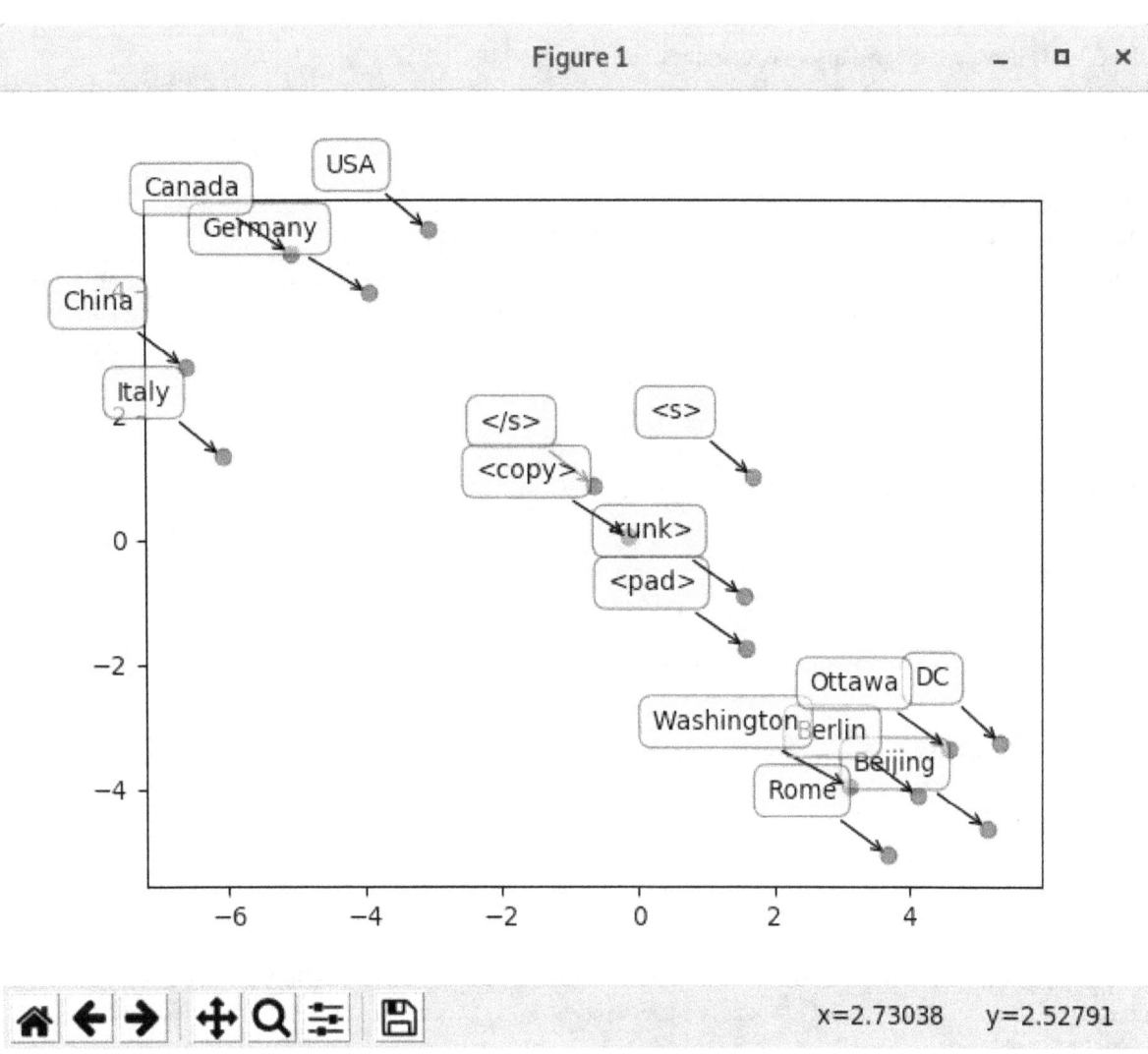

Figure 1.3: country city in the embedding space

In the graph above, we can clearly see that the countries are in one area, cities are in another area in the embedding output space. That is exactly what we want: similar words are located nearby in the embedding space.

1.2.4   Pre-trained word embedding: Word2vec/GloVe/BERT

Rather than training our own word vectors from scratch, we can leverage some pre-trained word embedding models.

Word2vec and GloVe are the two most popular ones.

1.2.4.1   Word2vec

Google's word2vec (https://code.google.com/archive/p/word2vec/) contains word vectors for a vocabulary of 3 million words, it was trained on around 100 billion words from the google news dataset.

According to https://en.wikipedia.org/wiki/Word2vec, it is a group of related models that are used to produce word embeddings. These models are shallow, two-layer neural networks that are trained to reconstruct linguistic contexts of words.

You can download it from: https://drive.google.com/file/d/0B7XkCwpI5KDYNlNUTTlSS21pQmM/edit

It is about 1.5 GB.

Usually, we can load it and start to use like the following:

```
import gensim

# if you vector file is in binary format, change to binary=True
model = gensim.models.Word2Vec.load_word2vec_format('path-to-vectors.txt', binary ↩
    =False)

sentence = ["Washing", "DC", "is", "the", "capital", "of", "USA"]

vectors = [model[w] for w in sentence]
```

1.2.4.2   GloVe

Another popular word embedding called Global Vectors for Word Representation (GloVe) was developed by Stanford researchers in 2014. (https://nlp.stanford.edu/projects/glove), it contains 400,000 English tokens trained from Wikipedia data.

PytorchNLP provides a good API to use it.

Tip

PytorchNLP also provides API to access other pre-trained embedding, for example: facebook's FastText, Byte-Pair Encoding (BPE) embedding etc. See more at:

https://pytorchnlp.readthedocs.io/en/latest/source/torchnlp.word_to_vector.html

---

Here is an example:

```
1  >>> from torchnlp.word_to_vector import GloVe
2  >>> vectors = GloVe()
3  >>> vectors['hello']
4  -1.7494
5  0.6242
6  ..
7  -0.6202
8  2.0928
9  [torch.FloatTensor of size 100]
```

1.2.4.3   Bidirectional Encoder Representations from Transformers (BERT)

BERT is a recent break-through in NLP, it can be used as word embedding. BERT offers an advantage over models like Word2Vec, because while each word has a fixed representation under Word2Vec regardless of the context within which the word appears, BERT produces word representations that are dynamically informed by the words around them. Please see the later section for more details.

In short, pre-trained word embeddings have been proven to be invaluable for improving performance in many natural language analysis tasks.

1.2.5   other applications for embedding layer

The embedding layer could be used in other areas (not just text processing).

Given the training data set, it can basically compress any sparse input space into a compact/structural space.

For example, to simulate online user behavior, we can assign indices to user behaviors like 'web page view on page X' or 'scrolled X pixels' etc, which are then used to construct a sequence of user behavior. By supplying a sequence of user behavior (as indices) as the input to an embedding layer of a model, We can capture/model those spatial(time) dimension information.

Another typical application is bioinformatics, where we can use an embedding layer to represent DNA, RNA, and Protein sequences, etc.

As long as we use indexes/integer as the input, we can use the embedding layer. So the possibilities of its application are unlimited, given the fact that we could assign arbitrary indexes to anything!

1.3 Language Translation - a seq2seq model application

One of the very interesting applications in NLP is language translation, it is a quite challenging problem.

Historically, people have tried several approaches with little success:

- example-based machine translation.

- rule-based approaches to machine translation

- statistical machine translation

In November 2016, Google switched to the neural machine translation engine (GNMT) for its translation services. It utilizes deep learning techniques to translate the whole sentences at a time, and ensures greater accuracy of the context, as shown in the following diagram.

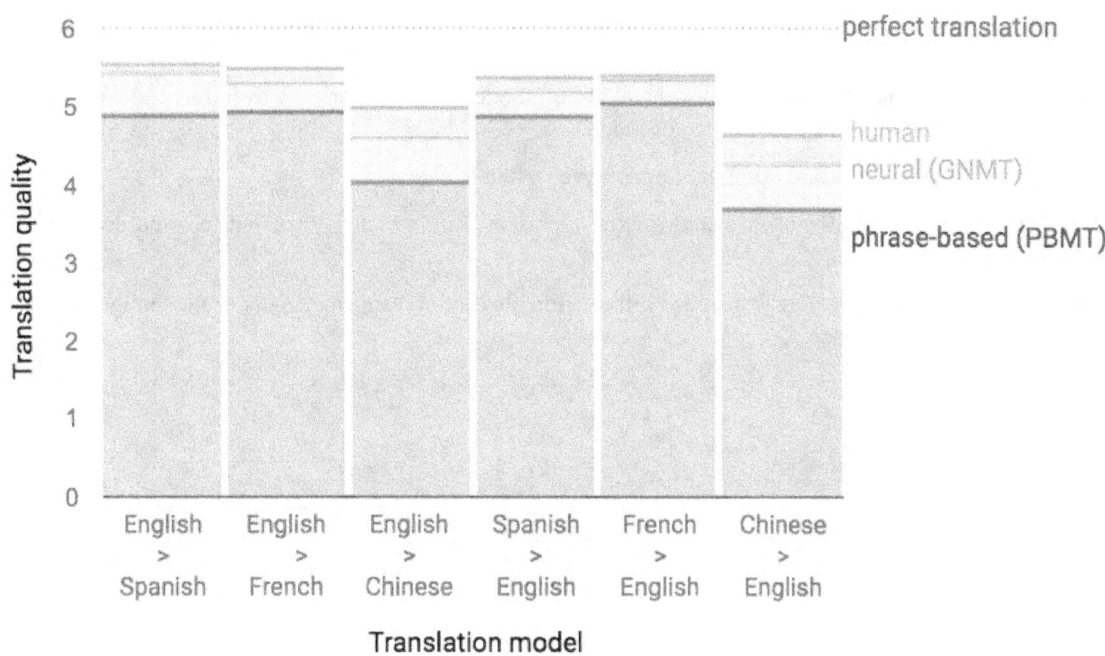

Figure 1.4: google translation quality using deep learning

BTW, GNMT supports over 100 languages at various levels, 200 million people used it daily.

Well, you may wonder how GNMT works?

Based on the documents released by google:
https://ai.googleblog.com/2016/09/a-neural-network-for-machine.html
https://arxiv.org/abs/1609.08144

We know it is based on a **sequence-to-sequence (seq2seq)** model. The only difference between GNMT and regular seq2seq model is that between the encoder and decoder there are 8 layers of LSTM-RNN that have residual connections between layers with some tweaks for accuracy and speed.

You can read more at:
https://blog.statsbot.co/machine-learning-translation-96f0ed8f19e4

In the section, we will try to explore this very useful seq2seq model.

First, we will try to understand how seq2seq works at a very high level, then, we will see a simplified example to show how the seq2seq model can be applied to language translation.

1.3.1 How seq2seq works

At very high level, a sequence-to-sequence model (seq2seq) model has an **encoder**, a **decoder**, and a connection called **thought vector** between the encoder and decoder.

Both the encoder and the decoder are normally implemented using RNN.

The encoder processes the input sequence into a fixed representation, which is then fed into the decoder as a context.

The decoder tries to use some previously decoded information plus a hint from an encoder or the thought vector to decode input to an output sequence.

1.3.1.1   training process

Seq2Seq Training Model

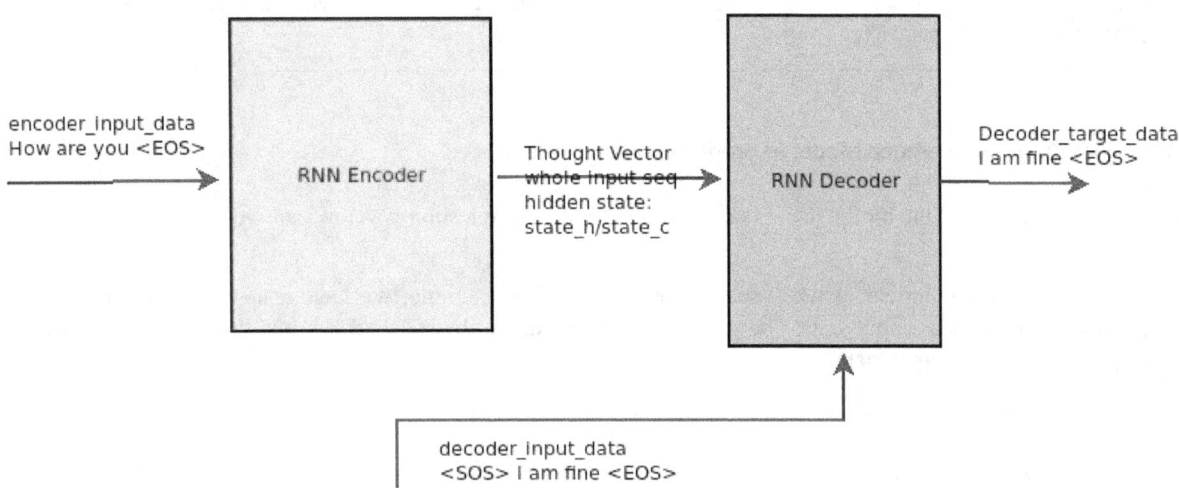

Figure 1.5: sequence-to-sequence model training process

The figure above showed the training process of a seq2seq model using RNN/LSTM as the encoder and decoder.

The basic idea is: we define a model (e.g: encoder + decoder), that can learn to generate 'targets[t+1...]' given 'targets[...t]', conditioned on the hint/thought vector. The thought vector is generated from the whole input sequence in the encoder initially.

Put another way, the initial hint is the encoder's RNN/lstm state in the last step, the hint after that will be decoder's RNN/lstm state from its previous step, please see more details when we do the code analysis in the sample code.

We could feed the following data to train the model:

[encoder_input_data, decoder_input_data] → decoder_target_data

Where encoder_input_data is the input sentence, e.g.: How are you, decoder_input_data is target data, e.g.: <SOS>I am fine.

decoder_target_data is what we want to generate: e.g.: I am fine

Please be noted decoder_input_data and decoder_target_data are NOT the same. **decoder_target_data is ahead of decoder_input_data by one timestep**. That is a key arrangement that enables us to use our model to predict/-generate the target based on the previous input.

Tip

The training method above is called **Teacher forcing**.
It uses the ground truth target outputs as the next input at each step, instead of using the decoder's predict as to the next input. Using teacher forcing causes the model to converge faster, but when the trained network is exploited, it may exhibit instability.

1.3.1.2   decoding: an inference model to predict/generate target

Assuming we have trained the model using teacher forcing, now the question is: How can we predict target data given an arbitrary input?

As we know, teacher forcing can not be used for prediction. For example, we have a new similar sentence, "how are you", thus encoder_input_data: "how are you", but we do not have decoder_input_data, so how can we generate/predict decoder_target_data?

Tip

In the teacher forcing training process, we had decoder_input_data information, since we know all the input and target output.

Some smart people come up with an **inference model** using the trained lstm encoder and decoder (meaning we use the same encoder/decoder to inference the target sequence) to predict target data.

The inference model looks like the following figure:

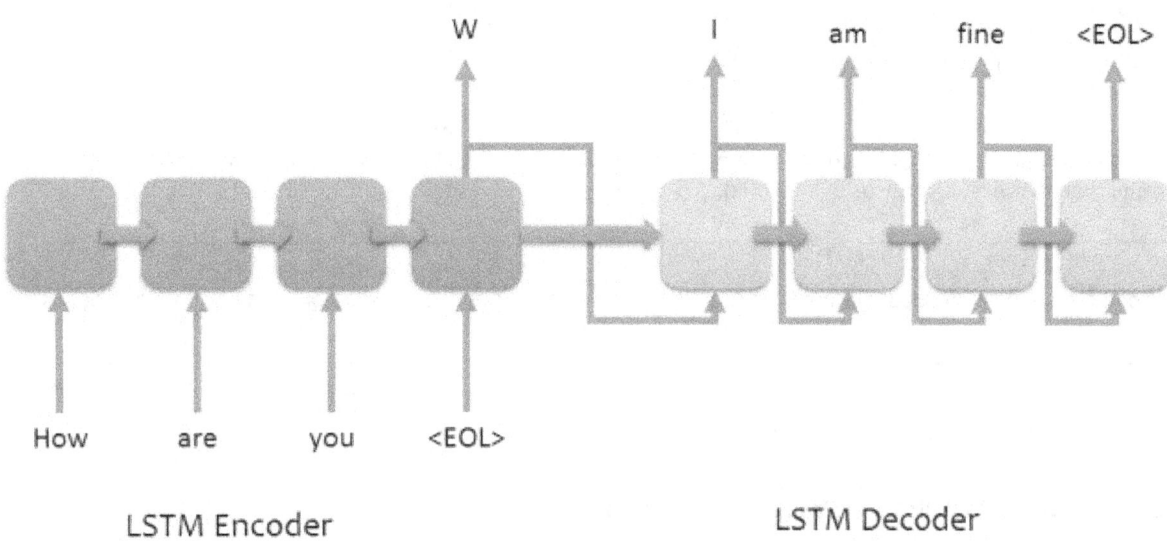

Figure 1.6: seq2seq decoding architecture

It works as following:

- We use the RNN encoder to encode the whole sequence (yes whole!), then feed the hidden state (last step's state_h/state_c) into RNN decoder as its initial hint, plus SOS symbol (start of the sequence) as the input, the decoder thus can decode the first word.

- Then we recursively feed the decoder's previous output and its new hidden state to predict the next target word. Here the encoder's hint was used only once (explicitly) !

One amaze thing about RNN networks is: lots of information can be compressed, stored and passed in the hidden state, after the proper training, and the initial hint can help to generate a whole target sequence, not just first word/character.

1.3.2   A language translation example using seq2seq model

The official pytorch web site provided an excellent example at:

https://pytorch.org/tutorials/intermediate/seq2seq_translation_tutorial.html

In this example, the traditional seq2seq model is enhanced with an **attention mechanism,** which force the decoder to learn to focus on a specific range of the input sequence.

Interesting readers should read this document, I simply do not want to repeat them in this book.

The whole source code can be downloaded at:

https://github.com/pytorch/tutorials/blob/master/intermediate_source/seq2seq_translation_tutorial.py

With the understanding of seq2seq from the previous section, I hope you can understand that example. It may take you some time to digest it, but worth doing that.

Tip

I welcome any question about the code, so that I could include the needed explanation in my next edition of this book.

In the section, I will highlight some key parts of the code.

1.3.2.1   language translation (seq2seq) training code analysis

The following code showed how the encoder/decoder is trained:

```
 1  teacher_forcing_ratio = 0.5
 2
 3  def train(input_tensor, target_tensor, encoder, decoder, encoder_optimizer,
 4  decoder_optimizer, criterion, max_length=MAX_LENGTH):
 5      encoder_hidden = encoder.initHidden()
 6
 7      encoder_optimizer.zero_grad()
 8      decoder_optimizer.zero_grad()
 9
10      input_length = input_tensor.size(0)
11      target_length = target_tensor.size(0)
12
13      encoder_outputs = torch.zeros(max_length, encoder.hidden_size, device=device)
14
15      loss = 0
16
```

```
17   for ei in range(input_length):
18       encoder_output, encoder_hidden = encoder(
19           input_tensor[ei], encoder_hidden)
20       encoder_outputs[ei] = encoder_output[0, 0]
21
22   decoder_input = torch.tensor([[SOS_token]], device=device)
23
24   decoder_hidden = encoder_hidden
25
26   use_teacher_forcing = True if random.random() < teacher_forcing_ratio else ↵
         False
27
28   if use_teacher_forcing:
29       # Teacher forcing: Feed the target as the next input
30       for di in range(target_length):
31           decoder_output, decoder_hidden, decoder_attention = decoder(
32               decoder_input, decoder_hidden, encoder_outputs)
33           loss += criterion(decoder_output, target_tensor[di])
34           decoder_input = target_tensor[di]  # Teacher forcing
35
36   else:
37       # Without teacher forcing: use its own predictions as the next input
38       for di in range(target_length):
39           decoder_output, decoder_hidden, decoder_attention = decoder(
40               decoder_input, decoder_hidden, encoder_outputs)
41           topv, topi = decoder_output.topk(1)
42           decoder_input = topi.squeeze().detach()  # detach from history as ↵
                 input
43
44           loss += criterion(decoder_output, target_tensor[di])
45           if decoder_input.item() == EOS_token:
46               break
47
48   loss.backward()
49
50   encoder_optimizer.step()
51   decoder_optimizer.step()
52
53   return loss.item() / target_length
```

The input_tensor is something like: le char est noir <EOS> The target_tensor is something like: the cat is black <EOS>

- Line 17 - 20, we use an encoder to encode the input_tensor.

- Line 22, we put <SOS> to decoder_input as a hint to start decoding.

- Line 24, the encoder_hidden was assigned to decoder_input, which will be used as a hint to the decoder initially. The encoder_hidden should contain all the info of the whole input_tensor for the decoder to decode it.

- Line 28 - 34 showed how we do the teacher forcing mode.
  Initially, in the first loop, decoder_input was SOS (from Line 22), decoder_hidden was encoder_hidden (from Line 24), we use that information to decode the first word. In the following loop, decoder_hidden was overwritten by Line 31, decoder_input was replaced by ground truth: target_tensor (Line 34) as we are using teacher forcing mode, then use this new information to decode again. The encoder_outputs is mainly used for attention calculation.

- Line 36 - 46 showed the code using non-teacher forcing mode, we need Line 45 to break the loop once the decoder_output (target_input) predict <EOS> token.

1.3.2.2 how to run seq2seq, and its running result

First, let's download the code and sample data.

```
1  # grab the source code
2  (pytorch-cpu) $ https://raw.githubusercontent.com/pytorch/tutorials/master/ ←
       intermediate_source/seq2seq_translation_tutorial.py
3
4  # download eng-fra.txt from:
5  # https://www.manythings.org/anki/fra-eng.zip
6  # unzip
7  (pytorch-cpu) $ unzip ../fra-eng.zip
8  Archive:  ../fra-eng.zip
9    inflating: _about.txt
10    inflating: fra.txt
11
12  (pytorch-cpu) mv fra.txt eng-fra.txt
```

Then, we can directly run it with pytorch environment, here is the result:

```
1  (pytorch-cpu) $ python seq2seq_translation_tutorial.py
2  Reading lines...
3  Read 160872 sentence pairs
4  Trimmed to 11974 sentence pairs
5  Counting words...
6  Counted words:
7  fra 4634
8  eng 2989
9  ['je ne suis toujours pas impressionnee .', 'i m still not impressed .']
10
11
12  16m 6s (- 225m 26s) (5000 6%) 2.8977
13  33m 27s (- 217m 26s) (10000 13%) 2.3339
14  49m 58s (- 199m 55s) (15000 20%) 2.0133
15  64m 35s (- 177m 37s) (20000 26%) 1.7958
16  79m 2s (- 158m 4s) (25000 33%) 1.5805
17  93m 30s (- 140m 16s) (30000 40%) 1.4558
18  108m 7s (- 123m 34s) (35000 46%) 1.3100
19  122m 46s (- 107m 25s) (40000 53%) 1.1906
20  137m 13s (- 91m 28s) (45000 60%) 1.0774
21  151m 45s (- 75m 52s) (50000 66%) 0.9776
22  166m 19s (- 60m 28s) (55000 73%) 0.8924
23  180m 57s (- 45m 14s) (60000 80%) 0.8504
24  195m 26s (- 30m 4s) (65000 86%) 0.7713
25  210m 1s (- 15m 0s) (70000 93%) 0.7199
26  224m 37s (- 0m 0s) (75000 100%) 0.6510
27  > c est un garcon tres gentil .
28  = he s a very nice boy .
29  < he s a very nice boy . <EOS>
30
31  > ils trainent les pieds .
32  = they re dragging their heels .
33  < they re enjoying their . <EOS>
34
35  > il est a tokyo .
36  = he s in tokyo .
37  < he is in tokyo . <EOS>
38
39  > je suis un puriste .
40  = i m a purist .
41  < i m a patient . <EOS>
```

```
42
43  > je suis familier du sujet .
44  = i m familiar with the subject .
45  < i am familiar with the problem . <EOS>
46
47  > ils sont conscients des difficultes .
48  = they are aware of the difficulties .
49  < they re out of the . <EOS>
50
51  > ce ne sont pas mes regles .
52  = they re not my rules .
53  < they re not my type . <EOS>
54
55  > nous ne sommes pas en train d acheter .
56  = we re not buying .
57  < we re not smiling . <EOS>
58
59  > je pense partir a la montagne .
60  = i am thinking of going to the mountains .
61  < i m thinking to play the . . <EOS>
62
63  > il a plutot raison .
64  = he is quite right .
65  < he is quite right . <EOS>
66
67  input = elle a cinq ans de moins que moi .
68  output = she is five years younger than me . <EOS>
69
70  input = elle est trop petit .
71  output = she is too a . <EOS>
72  input = je ne crains pas de mourir .
73  output = i m not scared of dying . <EOS>
74  input = c est un jeune directeur plein de talent .
75  output = he s a talented young player . <EOS>
```

The result is pretty good!

1.3.3   other applications for seq2seq model

A seq2seq model has a wide range of applications, including machine translation, image captioning, chatbot application etc.

In general, if input sequences and target output sequences have different length, or we need to use the entire input sequence to jump-start predicting the target, then seq2seq is probably a good choice.

1.4 Attention, Transformers, BERT

Seq2Seq model normally uses recurrent and convolutional layers to map one variable-length sequence of symbol representations to to another sequence of equal length, it was a state-of-the-art approach to handle sequence and transduction problems. However, the inherent sequential operation of RNNs precludes parallelization especially for longer sequence.

Tip

What is transduction?

According to Wikipedia: Transduction is reasoning from observed, specific (training) cases to specific (test) cases. In contrast, induction is reasoning from observed training cases to general rules, which are then applied to the test cases.

An self-attention based **transformer** was proposed to overcome the limitation in an influential paper called "Attention Is All You Need" in 2017:

https://arxiv.org/pdf/1706.03762.pdf

The transformer relies entirely on the attention mechanism to draw global dependencies between input and output, thus allows for significantly more parallelization.

In this section, we will introduce attention/transformers first, then we will see how it is applied to a break-through application BERT.

1.4.1 Attention, self-attention

An **attention** function can be described as mapping a query (Q) and a set of key-value (K, V) pairs to an output (attention), where the query, keys, values, and output are all vectors.

The output is computed as a weighted sum of the values, where the weight assigned to each value is computed by a compatibility function of the query with the corresponding key.

We can think it roughly like a SQL query in a database:

```
1  select birthday where name = "tom"
```

Birthday is the query content, the condition: name = "tom" is the key-value pair, the database will return an output based on this SQL query.

The training process of an attention layer will teach the network how to output relevant attention/score for our specific problem.

In an **self-attention** (also called **intra-attention**) layer, all of the keys, values and queries come from the same space.

There are two types of self-attention, shown as the following figure:

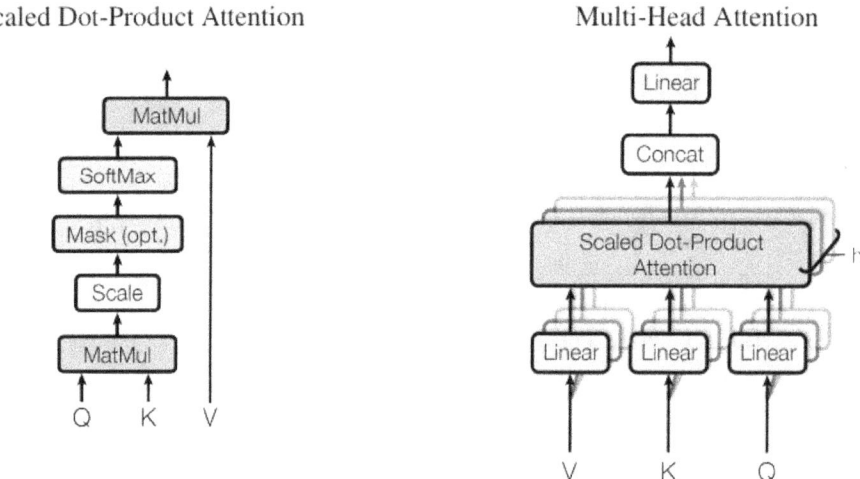

Figure 1.7: (left) Scaled Dot-Product Attention. (right) Multi-Head Attention consists of several attention layers running in parallel

The first one is called **Scaled Dot-Product Attention**, where we compute the dot products of the query with all keys, divide each by d_k, and apply a softmax function to obtain the weights on the values, where d_k is the dimension of K. Mathematically, we can write it as:

$$\text{Attention}(Q, K, V) = \text{softmax}(\frac{QK^T}{\sqrt{d_k}})V$$

Figure 1.8: Scaled Dot-Product Attention

The second one is called **Multi-Head Attention**, where we first linearly project Q, K, V into a different space, then apply the previous Scaled Dot-Product Attention there, we do it h times (with different projections) as it is shown in the diagram.

The following table showed the benefits of using self-attention layer compared to the Recurrent and Convolutional layer. For example, an self-attention layer connects all positions with a constant number of sequentially executed operations, whereas a recurrent layer requires O(n) sequential operations. For tasks involving very long sequences, self-attention could be restricted to considering only a neighborhood of size r in the input sequence centered around the respective output position.

Table 1: Maximum path lengths, per-layer complexity and minimum number of sequential operations for different layer types. n is the sequence length, d is the representation dimension, k is the kernel size of convolutions and r the size of the neighborhood in restricted self-attention.

Layer Type	Complexity per Layer	Sequential Operations	Maximum Path Length
Self-Attention	$O(n^2 \cdot d)$	$O(1)$	$O(1)$
Recurrent	$O(n \cdot d^2)$	$O(n)$	$O(n)$
Convolutional	$O(k \cdot n \cdot d^2)$	$O(1)$	$O(log_k(n))$
Self-Attention (restricted)	$O(r \cdot n \cdot d)$	$O(1)$	$O(n/r)$

Figure 1.9: self-attention layer comparing to Recurrent and Convolutional layer

Another side benefit of self-attention is it could yield more interpretable models.

The following figure may give you some idea what attention looks like, for a word sequence problem, not only do individual attention heads clearly learn to perform different tasks, many appear to exhibit behavior related to the syntactic and semantic structure of the sentences.

attention visualization for multiple heads, many of the attention heads exhibit behavior that seems related to the structure of the sentence. We give two such examples above, from two different heads from the encoder self-attention at layer 5 of 6. The heads clearly learned to perform different tasks. :images/attention_visualization_multi_head

1.4.2 Positional Encoding

Another important technique in the transformer model is **positional encoding**, which makes use of the order of a sequence. It provides some information about the relative or absolute position of the tokens in the sequence.

There are many choices of positional encodings, either learned or fixed, the following showed one way to do it:

$$PE_{(pos,2i)} = sin(pos/10000^{2i/d_{model}})$$
$$PE_{(pos,2i+1)} = cos(pos/10000^{2i/d_{model}})$$

Figure 1.10: positional encoding sine and cosine functions of different frequencies

where pos is the position and i is the dimension, d_{model} is the dimensionality of input and output. That is, each dimension of the positional encoding corresponds to a sinusoid.

Finally, we will add those positional encodings to the input embeddings at the bottoms of the encoder and decoder stacks in transformer's architecture.

The positional encodings have the same dimension dmodel as the embeddings, so that the two can be summed.

1.4.3 Transformers

With all the above background knowledge, we can understand transformers now.

The **transformer** is the first transduction model relying entirely on self-attention to compute representations of its input and output without using sequence aligned RNNs or convolution.

The architecture of transformer is shown as following diagram:

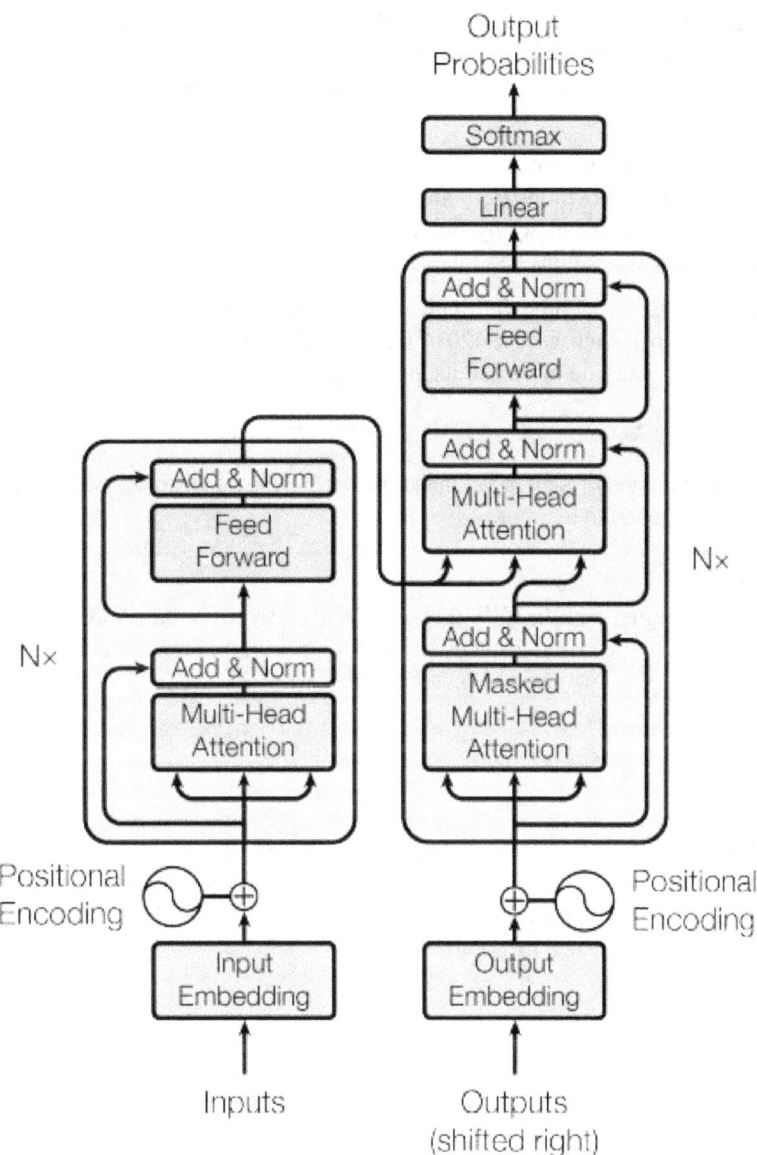

Figure 1.11: transformer architecture

It is quite similar to a seq2seq model, it has an encoder, decoder.

The encoder is composed of a stack of N (e.g.: 6) identical layers. Each layer has two sub-layers. The first is a multi-head self-attention mechanism, and the second is a simple, position-wise fully connected feed-forward network. Also it has a residual connection around each of the two sub-layers, followed by layer normalization. In the original paper, all layers produce outputs of dimension dmodel = 512.

Similarly, the decoder is also composed of a stack of (e.g.: 6) identical layers. In addition to the two sub-layers in each encoder layer, the decoder inserts a third sub-layer, which performs multi-head attention over the output of the encoder stack. Similar to the encoder, there are residual connections around each of the sub-layers, followed by layer normalization.

Please be noted that the self-attention sub-layer in the decoder stack is different from the encoder's counterpart. It is modified with a masking to prevent positions from attending to subsequent positions. This masking, combined with fact that the output embeddings are offset by one position, ensures that the predictions for position i can depend only on the known outputs at positions less than i.

The transformer achieves better BLEU scores than previous state-of-the-art machine translation models on the English-to-German and English-to-French newstest2014 tests at **a fraction of the training cost** (about 1/10 or 1/100 FLOPS). Interested readers can find more details in the paper.

Tip
BLEU (bilingual evaluation understudy) is an algorithm for evaluating the quality of text which has been machine-translated from one natural language to another.

In short, **transformer can be trained significantly faster than architectures based on recurrent or convolutional layers**. It has become the basic building block of most state-of-the-art architectures in NLP/Time series areas etc.

Google open sourced its transformers at:
https://github.com/tensorflow/tensor2tensor

1.4.4 Bidirectional Encoder Representations from Transformers (BERT)

One of the recent break-through using Transformer in language model/NLP is Bidirectional Encoder Representations from Transformers (BERT), published by google at 2019:
https://arxiv.org/pdf/1810.04805.pdf

Google open source its code is at:+ https://github.com/google-research/bert

The paper claimed new state-of-the-art results on eleven natural language processing tasks using pre-trained BERT, including pushing the GLUE score to 80.5% (7.7% point absolute improvement), MultiNLI accuracy to 86.7% (4.6% absolute improvement), SQuAD v1.1 question answering Test F1 to 93.2 (1.5 point absolute improvement) and SQuAD v2.0 Test F1 to 83.1.

Comparing to those famous **context-free** word-embedding models such as word2vec and GloVe, which generate a single word embedding representation regardless context, BERT is a **contextual model**, which generates a representation of each word that is based on the other words in the sentence.

What are the benefits of a contextual model?

Let's look at an example:
I like to eat apples.
I like Apple's iphone.

We can easily see that the word apple has a different semantic meaning in each sentence. With a contextualized language model, the embedding of the word apple would have a different vector representation, thus makes it even more suitable for NLP tasks.

One unique feature of BERT, which distinguishes it from other unidirectional or shallowly bidirectional contextual models (e.g.: Generative Pre-Training, ELMo, the OpenAI Transformer, ULMFit), is that it is fully bidirectional, and can captures these relationships in a bidirectional way.

1.4.4.1 BERT architecture

BERT architecture is actually quite simple!

Since BERT's goal is to generate a language model, it only makes use of the encoder mechanism from the Transformer architecture. Thus **it is just the transformer's encoders part**!

The paper primarily report resulted on two model sizes:

- BERTBASE (L=12, H=768, A=12, Total Parameters=110M)

- BERTLARGE (L=24, H=1024,A=16, Total Parameters=340M)

In short, BERT is basically a trained Transformer encoder stack, with 12 layers in the Base version, and 24 layers in the Large version, compared to 6 encoder layers in the original Transformer.

1.4.4.2   how BERT is pre-trained

BERT will be trained using two unsupervised tasks: masked language model and next sentence prediction.

We will first look at the wordPiece embeddings and BERT input representation, then we will introduce masked language model and next Sentence Prediction, finally we will see how we can hook all those together to pre-train a BERT model.

1.4.4.3   WordPiece Model (WPM)

BERT uses **WordPiece embeddings** with a 30,000 token vocabulary.

What is WordPiece embedding?

It divides words into a limited set of common sub-word units called wordpieces to improve handling of rare words,

For example:
Word: Jet makers feud over seat width with big orders at stake
wordpieces: _J et _makers _fe ud _over _seat _width _with _big _orders _at _stake

In the above example, the word "Jet" is broken into two wordpieces "_J" and "et", and the word "feud" is broken into two wordpieces "_fe" and "ud". The other words remain as single wordpieces. "_" is a special character added to mark the beginning of a word.

As you can see, this method provides a good balance between the flexibility of "character"-delimited models and the efficiency of "word"-delimited models. Also it can handle open vocabularies and the challenge of morphologically rich languages effectively.

Of course, there are more details that need to be considered, but you get the idea.

Interested readers can read more at:
https://arxiv.org/pdf/1609.08144.pdf

1.4.4.4   BERT input representation

Let's look at the BERT input representation in more detail.

In BERT, a **sentence** can be an arbitrary span of contiguous text, rather than an actual linguistic sentence, and it will be converted into WordPeiece tokens.

A **sequence** refers to the input token sequence to BERT, which may be a single sentence or two sentences packed together.

BERT also defined several rules:

- The first token of every sequence is always a special classification token ([CLS]).

- Sentence pairs are packed together into a single sequence. The are separated with a special token ([SEP]).

- A learned embedding to every token indicating whether it belongs to sentence A or sentence B (as shown Segment Embeddings below) is used.

The following figure may give you better idea what BERT input looks like:

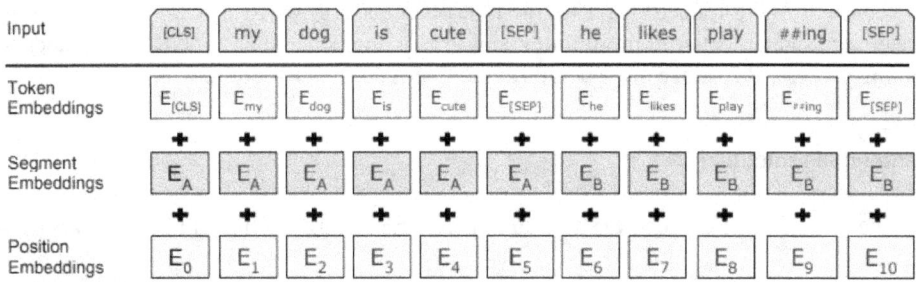

Figure 1.12: The input embeddings are the sum of the token embeddings, the segmentation embeddings and the position embeddings

As shown in the figure above, for a given token, its input representation is constructed by summing the corresponding token, segment, and position embeddings.

1.4.4.5 Masked language model (MLM)

Now we can talk about how BERT was trained.

The first technique is called: **masked language model (MLM) (also referred as cloze task)**, it randomly masks some of the tokens from the input, and the objective is to predict the original vocabulary id of the masked word based only on its context.

Unlike left-to-right language model pre-training, the MLM objective enables the representation to fuse the left and the right context, which allows us to train a deep bidirectional Transformer.

That fits our intuition, remember the fill-in-the-blanks sentences exercises from our childhood, we need to look at words/context around that blank (bidirectional context) in order to figure out which word to be filled in.

Please be noted that the BERT MLM loss function takes into consideration only the prediction of the masked values and ignores the prediction of the non-masked words.

In BERT, the training data generator chooses 15% of the token positions at random for prediction, but it will not replace all of them with [MASK] token. Instead, BERT replaces the chosen tokens with:

- the [MASK] token 80% of the time

- a random token 10% of the time

- the unchanged i-th token 10% of the time.

Why?

The reason is we want to use a pre-trained BERT to fine-tune other tasks. If we replace all the token with [MASK] token, we will create a mismatch between pre-training and fine-tuning, since the [MASK] token does not appear during the fine-tuning process. Please see more details at the fine-tune BERT section.

1.4.4.6 Next Sentence Prediction (NSP)

The second technique is the **Next Sentence Prediction**, where BERT learns to model relationships between sentences.

Specifically, when choosing the sentences A and B for each training example, 50% of the time B is the actual next sentence that follows A (labeled as IsNext), and 50% of the time it is a random sentence from the corpus (labeled as NotNext).

What are the benefits of doing this?

Well, many important downstream tasks such as Question Answering (QA) and Natural Language Inference (NLI) are based on understanding the relationship between two sentences, with NSP pre-training, BERT can be used for those tasks, the paper showed it is very beneficial to both QA and NLI.

1.4.4.7 BERTBASE and BERTLARGE

Powered by those two techniques, BERT can be pre-trained on a large corpus of unlabelled text which includes the entire Wikipedia (that's about 2,500 million words) and a book corpus (800 million words).

The paper trained two models with different settings:

- BERTBASE (L=12, H=768, A=12, Total Parameters=110M)

- BERTLARGE (L=24, H=1024, A=16, Total Parameters=340M)

Where L denotes: Number of transformer blocks
H: Hidden layer size
A: Attention heads

BERT shines when it is applied to many NLP downstream tasks. The original paper presented BERT fine-tuning results on 11 NLP tasks.

1.4.5   How to apply BERT to downstream tasks

As we know, BERT is a context-sensitive word representation/embedding, so we can use it just the way like other word-embeddings.

Specifically, we can fine-tune BERT with other tasks/models or simply use the pre-trained BERT as a bottleneck feature-extractor.

Some typical NLP tasks are:

- **Named Entity Recognition (NER)**: which words in a sentence are a proper name, organization name, or entity?
  For example, the model receives a text sequence and is required to mark the various types of entities (Person, Organization, Date, etc) that appear in the text.

- **Textual Entailment**: given two sentences, does the first sentence entail or contradict the second sentence?

- **Coreference Resolution**: given a pronoun like "it" in a sentence that discusses multiple objects, which object does "it" refer to?

- **Question Answering** tasks: the model receives a question regarding a text sequence and is required to mark the answer in the sequence.

. . .

The following are some famous NLP datasets for those tasks:

- GLUe: General Language Understanding Evaluation, a collection of resources for training,evaluating, and analyzing natural language understanding systems, more at:
  https://gluebenchmark.com/

- SQuAD v1.1: Stanford Question Answering Dataset, is a collection of 100k crowdsourced question/answer pairs.

- SQuAD 2.0: It extends the SQuAD 1.1 problem definition by allowing for the possibility that no short answer exists in the provided paragraph, making the problem more realistic. More at:
  https://rajpurkar.github.io/SQuAD-explorer/

- SWAG: The Situations With Adversarial Generations dataset contains 113k sentence-pair completion examples that evaluate grounded common sense inference. Given a sentence, the task is to choose the most plausible continuation among four choices. More at:
  https://rowanzellers.com/swag/

1.4.5.1 fine-tune BERT

The way to do fine-tuning is to add a simple classification layer to the pre-trained model, then all parameters will be jointly fine-tuned on a downstream task.

The following diagram showed the overall pre-training and fine-tuning procedures for BERT.

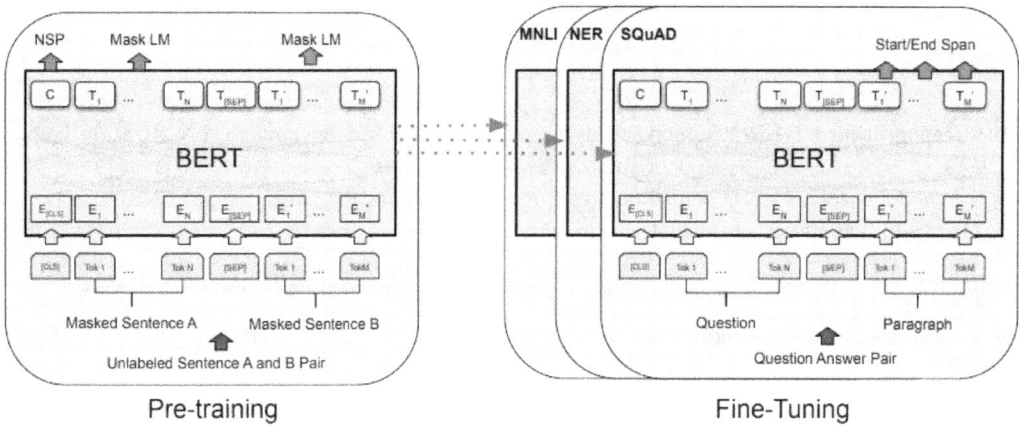

Figure 1.13: Overall pre-training and fine-tuning procedures for BERT

Apart from output layers, the same architectures are used in both pre-training and fine-tuning. The same pre-trained model parameters are used to initialize models for different down-stream tasks. During fine-tuning, all parameters are fine-tuned. [CLS] is a special symbol added in front of every input example, and [SEP] is a special separator token (e.g. separating questions/answers).

For example:

- For classification tasks such as sentiment analysis, we can do those like Next Sentence classification by adding a classification layer on top of the Transformer output for the [CLS] token.

- For Question Answering tasks (e.g. SQuAD v1.1), a Q&A model can be trained with BERT by learning two extra vectors that mark the beginning and the end of the answer.

- For Named Entity Recognition, a NER model with BERT can be trained by feeding the output vector of each token into a classification layer that predicts the NER label.

Please see the original paper for more details.

1.4.5.2   BERT feature extraction

Another way to use BERT is the feature-based approach, where fixed features are extracted from the pre-trained model.

This approach is much simpler and easier to use than fine-tuning, and has major computational benefits.

BERT base model has 12 layers of transformer encoders, each output per token from each layer of these can be used as a word embedding!

The paper reported that the best performing method is to concatenate the token representations from the **top four hidden layers** of the pre-trained Transformer. The performance (accuracy etc.) is only a little behind the fine-tuning.

1.4.6   RoBERTa, DistilBERT, XLNet

There are several improvements on BERT since its inception in 2018/2019. The following are just some of them:

- **RoBERTa**, Robustly optimized BERT approach from Facebook, found that BERT was significantly under-trained, so they retrain the BERT with following improvements:
  (1) training the model longer, with bigger batches, over more data;
  (2) removing the next sentence prediction objective;

(3) training on longer sequences;

(4) dynamically changing the masking pattern applied to the training data.

More details at:

https://arxiv.org/abs/1907.11692

- **DistilBERT**, is a distilled (approximate) version of BERT, retaining 97% performance but using only half the number of parameters (paper), improves on the inference speed. More at

  https://arxiv.org/abs/1910.01108

- **XLNet**, is a large bidirectional transformer based on generalized autoregressive pretraining method. The authors of XLNet believe that BERT neglects dependency between the masked positions by only relying on corrupting the input with masks, thus suffers from a pretrain-finetune discrepancy. So they improve BERT by:

  (1) enables learning bidirectional contexts by maximizing the expected likelihood over all permutations of the factorization order.

  (2) overcomes the limitations of BERT thanks to its autoregressive formulation.

  (3) XLNet integrates ideas from Transformer-XL, the state-of-the-art autoregressive model, into pretraining.

  More at:

  https://arxiv.org/abs/1906.08237

	BERT	RoBERTa	DistilBERT	XLNet
Size (millions)	**Base**: 110 **Large**: 340	**Base**: 110 **Large**: 340	**Base**: 66	**Base**: ~110 **Large**: ~340
Training Time	**Base**: 8 x V100 x 12 days* **Large**: 64 TPU Chips x 4 days (or 280 x V100 x 1 days*)	**Large**: 1024 x V100 x 1 day; 4-5 times more than BERT.	**Base**: 8 x V100 x 3.5 days; 4 times less than BERT.	**Large**: 512 TPU Chips x 2.5 days; 5 times more than BERT.
Performance	Outperforms state-of-the-art in Oct 2018	2-20% improvement over BERT	3% degradation from BERT	2-15% improvement over BERT
Data	16 GB BERT data (Books Corpus + Wikipedia). 3.3 Billion words.	160 GB (16 GB BERT data + 144 GB additional)	16 GB BERT data. 3.3 Billion words.	**Base**: 16 GB BERT data **Large**: 113 GB (16 GB BERT data + 97 GB additional). 33 Billion words.
Method	BERT (Bidirectional Transformer with MLM and NSP)	BERT without NSP**	BERT Distillation	Bidirectional Transformer with Permutation based modeling

Figure 1.14: Comparison of BERT and recent improvements over it

In short, XLNet and RoBERTa improve on the performance while DistilBERT improves on the inference speed.

1.4.7 Transformer/BERT code examples

Enough theory, how can we apply transformers, BERT to real life projects?

Fortunately there are some pretty good open source transformer libraries.

The most famous one is:

https://github.com/huggingface/transformers

This lib has lots of features, provides the following tasks pre-trained model out of the box:

- Sentiment analysis: is a text positive or negative?

- Text generation (in English): provide a prompt and the model will generate what follows.

- Name entity recognition (NER): in an input sentence, label each word with the entity it represents (person, place, etc.)

- Question answering: provide the model with some context and a question, extract the answer from the context.

- Filling masked text: given a text with masked words (e.g., replaced by [MASK]), fill the blanks.

- Summarization: generate a summary of a long text.

- Translation: translate a text in another language.

- Feature extraction: return a tensor representation of the text.

The easiest way to use a pretrained model on a given task is to use pipeline().

Huggingface provided excellent documents at:
https://huggingface.co/transformers/quicktour.html
https://huggingface.co/transformers/task_summary.html
https://huggingface.co/transformers/main_classes/pipelines.html
https://huggingface.co/transformers/

I will let you to explore those documents instead of duplicating their documents here.

I could not find a feature-extraction example from their documents, so here is one for your references.

Let's use google colab.

```
1  !pip install transformers
2  from transformers import pipeline
3
4  # let's use it as feature extraction
5  nlp = pipeline('feature-extraction')
6
7  # check its model
8  nlp.model
9  DistilBertModel(
10   (embeddings): Embeddings(
11     (word_embeddings): Embedding(28996, 768, padding_idx=0)
12     (position_embeddings): Embedding(512, 768)
```

```
13      (LayerNorm): LayerNorm((768,), eps=1e-12, elementwise_affine=True)
14      (dropout): Dropout(p=0.1, inplace=False)
15    )
16    (transformer): Transformer(
17      (layer): ModuleList(
18  ...
19
20  # check its tokenizer
21  nlp.tokenizer
22  <transformers.tokenization_distilbert.DistilBertTokenizer at 0x7fcac109b7f0>
23
24  # let's get nlp feature
25  feature1 = nlp("This is a dog.")
26
27  # the feature1 will be python list
28  # feature1
29  [[[0.5429945588111877,
30     0.06277535110712051,
31     0.01794254407286644,
32     -0.3357508182525635,
33     -0.21964314579963684,
34     -0.05832929536700249,
35  ...
36  ]]]
37
38  # get length of output
39  print(len(feature1[0]))
40  > 7
41
42  # get len of features for the token at [1]
43  # print(feature1[0][1])
44  768
45
46  # we can specify a model/token for this feature-extract pipeline
47  model = BertModel.from_pretrained('bert-base-uncased')
48  tokenizer_fast = BertTokenizerFast.from_pretrained('bert-base-uncased',
49  add_special_tokens=False)
50  nlp2 = pipeline('feature-extraction', model=model, tokenizer=tokenizer_fast, ↩
        device=0)
51
52  featuers2 = nlp2('This is a dog.')
53
```

```
54   # we can convert the list to pytorch tensor
55   import torch
56   t = torch.tensor(features2)
57   t.shape
58   torch.Size([1, 7, 768])
```

Once we get features, we can use it for any other NLP tasks.

https://huggingface.co/transformers/task_summary.html listed many other interesting examples, please read it.

1.4.8   Useful References

https://modelzoo.co/model/pytorch-pretrained-bert

https://github.com/codertimo/BERT-pytorch

https://www.tensorflow.org/tutorials/text/transformer

https://towardsdatascience.com/bert-classifier-just-another-pytorch-model-881b3cf05784

https://towardsdatascience.com/bert-roberta-distilbert-xlnet-which-one-to-use-3d5ab82ba5f8

https://towardsdatascience.com/understanding-bert-is-it-a-game-changer-in-nlp-7cca943cf3ad

1.5   Language understanding - Digital assistant, Answer bot, Chat bot

Another typical/popular application in NLP is: digital assistant, chatbot, question/answer(QA or FAQ) bot such as google home, and amazon's echo, etc.

Figure 1.15: amazon's echo (chatbot)

To build such an end-to-end system includes many fields: speech recognition, natural language understanding, and natural language generation, etc. Any of the fields above are quite challenging.

In this section, we will focus only on natural language understanding and generation.

In the early days (before the 1980s), many language-processing systems were **rule-based** systems, which were designed by hand-coding a set of rules, e.g. by writing grammars or devising heuristic rules for stemming. However, this is rarely robust to natural language variation.

In the late 1980s and mid-1990s, many NLP research started to use statistical models, thus heavily rely on machine learning techniques.

Recently, deep learning made the road into Language understanding without surprise.

We will try to see how DL is applied to language understanding under the chat framework.

First, we will briefly introduce how a chatbot is implemented. Then, we will spend a lot of effort to try to understand the promising memory network model for language understanding.

1.5.1   a classification type of chat bot

There are many ways to implement a chatbot.

A very simple chatbot system could be built by turning a chatbot problem into a classification problem.

The rough idea is: we can classify a question/sentence into one type of intent, then generate an answer from a predefined answer set.

For example, we could group the followings as one type/intent of greeting:
Hi,
Hello,
How are you?

Then we can generate an answer for that greeting from a predefined set:
I am fine,
how about you?
Hi

A more concrete example can be found at:

https://blog.eduonix.com/internet-of-things/simple-nlp-based-chatbot-python/

You probably noticed its limitations: not all the questions could be easily classified as intents!

1.5.2   seq-2-seq chat bot

A more sophisticated chatbot could be implemented by a classic Encoder-Decoder (seq2seq) model we learned before.

Again, the official pytorch website provides an excellent example at:

https://pytorch.org/tutorials/beginner/chatbot_tutorial.html

While seq2seq models can theoretically solve QA problems, their performance is limited by the small size of their 'memory', as seq2seq models or any RNN model tend to encode all information into one dense/fixed-length vector (encoded as hidden states and weights), then pass it between encoder and decoder, thus is not compartmentalized enough to accurately remember facts from the past.

Imagining use cases where we have very long sequences of data (videos, books, long stories, etc), the limitation becomes apparent, especially when the very facts may occur a long time apart.

So smart people tried to mitigate this limitation by storing multiple hidden states, and then using a strategy called an **attention** mechanism to choose between them. Those models are normally referred to as **memory network** models.

It is a novel and exciting way of doing language understanding and comprehension. We will explore this in the next section.

1.5.3   memory network model based chat bot or Auto FAQ

Let's imagine for a moment how human beings talk and chat, how people raise questions and answers.

Normally, we need some sort of comprehension. Based on our understanding of content, we can answer a question. The key is understanding!

If the computer has the reading comprehension just like a human being, implementing a chatbot or FAQ is quite a simple task, right?

Unfortunately, reading comprehension is, actually, one of holy grail, the hardest problems in NLP.

Recent deep learning progresses shed some light on this.

Facebook **bAbi** (https://research.fb.com/downloads/babi/) is a project towards the goal of automatic text understanding and reasoning. It released a very useful synthetic dataset that can help evaluate reading comprehension systems.

The datasets consist of:

- The (20) QA bAbI tasks

- The (6) dialog bAbI tasks

- The Children's Book Test

- The Movie Dialog dataset

- The WikiMovies dataset

- The Dialog-based Language Learning dataset

- The SimpleQuestions dataset

- HITL Dialogue Simulator

Tip

Why synthetic dataset?

Short answer, we do not know how to solve this general problem.

Longer answer: real world data is noisy. It rarely provides a clear and simple answer for you to train on. Additionally, even a well curated dataset from the real world is littered with nuance, complexities, and errors.

---

bAbI tasks were first evaluated on an LSTM-based system, which achieved only 50% performance on average and did not pass any task.

Weston et al. is probably the first team to propose a novel memory networks to handle bAbI tasks in 2014.

The memory network architecture looks like the following:

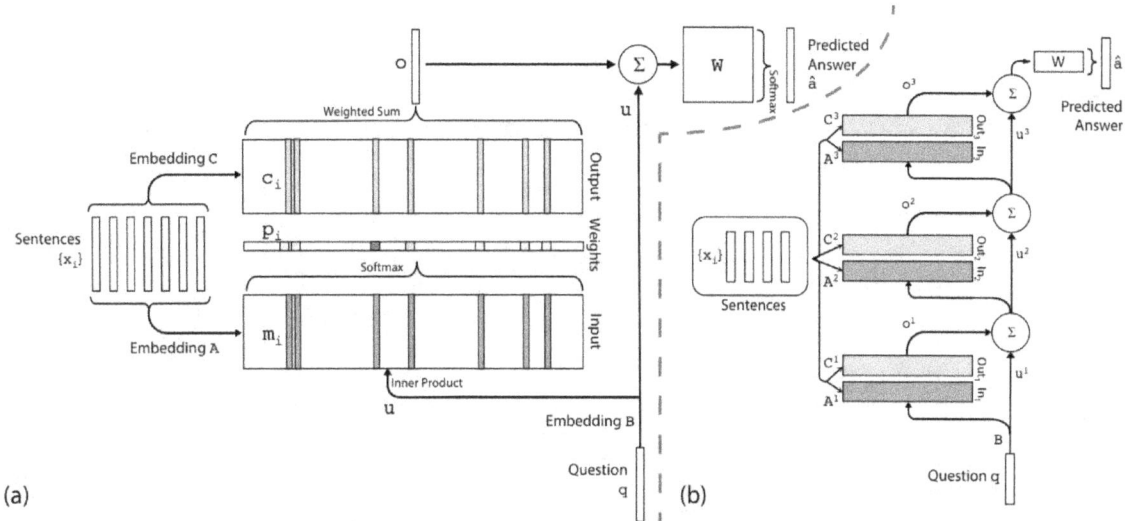

Figure 1: (a): A single layer version of our model. (b): A three layer version of our model. In practice, we can constrain several of the embedding matrices to be the same (see Section 2.2).

Figure 1.16: memory network model diagram

It is a recurrent network, has a long-term memory component where it can learn to write some data (the input sentences) and read them later. We will not dig into the details here. Interesting readers can read its original paper at: https://arxiv.org/abs/1410.3916 (published in 2014).

Later, Kumar et al. (2015) from Metamind proposed **Dynamic Memory Network (DMN)** in https://arxiv.org/abs/1506.07285.

DMN is more general than previous memory network models, it could be applied to many other interesting areas.

In the next few sections, we will dig into more details of DMN.

1.5.3.1   How Dynamic Memory Network works?

In short, DMN is a neural network architecture optimized for question-answering (QA) problems. Given a training set of input sequences (knowledge) and questions, it can form episodic memories, and use them to generate relevant answers.

It refines the attention mechanism so that questions trigger an iterative attention process, which allows the model to condition its attention on the inputs and the result of previous iterations.

DMN architecture has the following components:

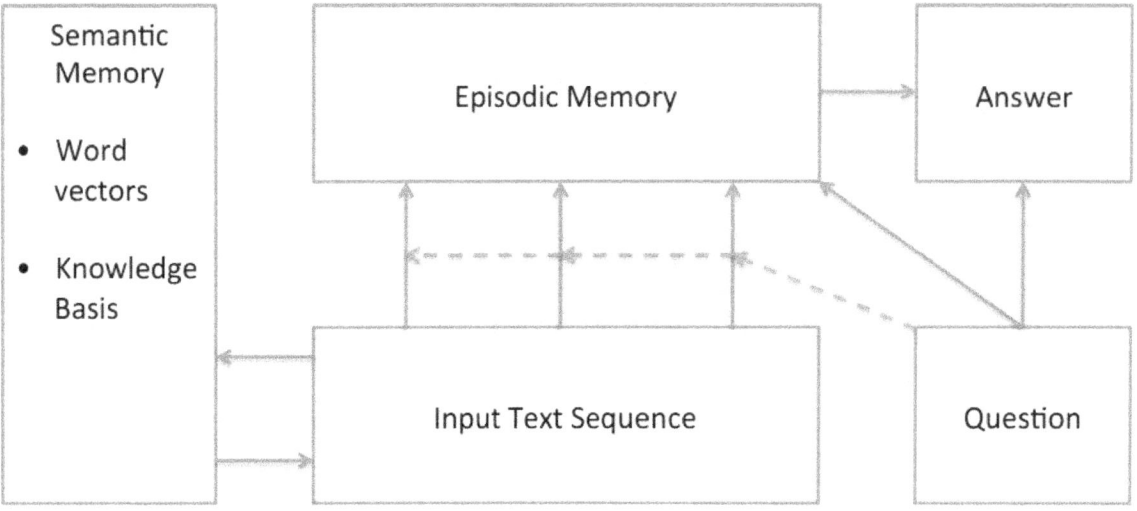

Figure 1.17: Dynamic Memory Network architecture

- The **Input Module** encodes raw text inputs (e.g. a long story etc.) into distributed vector representations. This module could be implemented using a GRU, which enables the network to learn if the sentence currently under consideration is relevant or nothing to do with the answer.

- The **Question Module**, like its input module, encodes the question into a distributed vector representation. It outputs a vector using the same GRU as the input module, and the same weights. Both facts and questions are encoded as embeddings.

- The **Semantic Memory Module** (analogous to a knowledge base) consists of pre-trained GloVe vectors that are used to create sequences of word embeddings from input sentences. These vectors will act as inputs to the model.

- The **Episodic Memory Module** receives the fact and question vectors extracted from the input and encoded as embeddings. In its general form, the episodic memory module is comprised of an attention mechanism as well as a recurrent network with which it updates its memory.

This is the key part of this model. It works as following:

The initial state of this GRU inside the memory is initialized to the question vector itself.

Then the module loops all the facts, computes the attention based on (question, memory). Essentially, we will get a vector [fact, attention].

What is the **attention**?
It approximately can be thought of as a score [0,1], which measures the relationship between fact and question. If it is 0, it means they are not related at all. If it is 1, that means they are very relevant, we should take this fact to do further reasoning.

Then, we use a GRU to generate episode = GRU([fact, attention]). As we know, GRU generates hint, we store all these GRUs' hints (episodes) into the memory.

Because of the updated memory, the attention may give different scores to the facts. So we need to and can do this step multiple times.

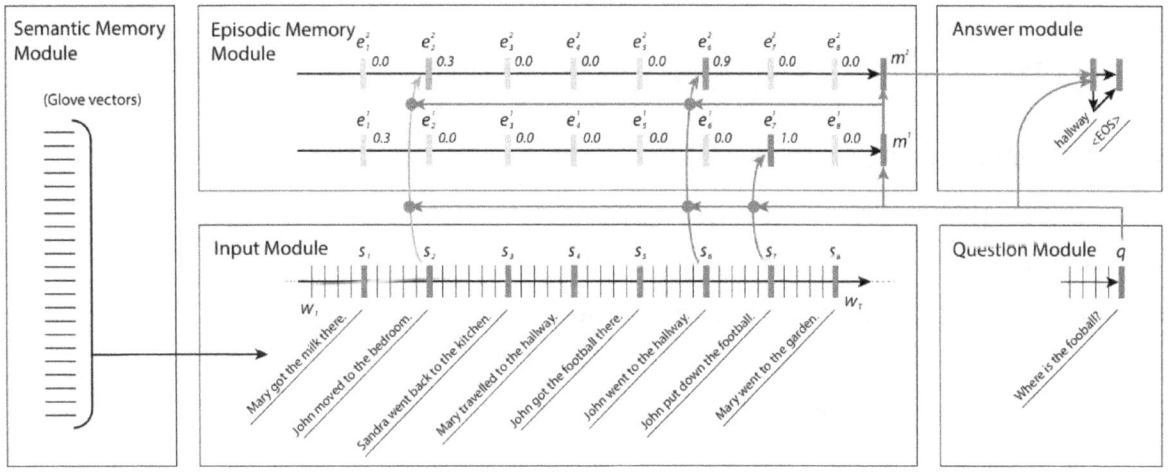

Figure 1.18: Details of Dynamic Memory Network

Quote from the original paper:
The iterative nature of this module allows it to attend to different inputs during each pass. It also allows for a type of transitive inference, since the first pass may uncover the need to retrieve additional facts.

Let's look at the example shown in the figure above, we are asked: "Where is the football?"

In the first iteration, the model ought to attend to sentence 7 (John put down the football.), because the question asks about the football. Please see the s7,e7 in the figure.

Once the model sees that John is relevant, it reasons that it should retrieve where John was in the second iteration. Similarly, a second pass/iteration will help for further sentiment analysis. See s6,e6 in the figure.

Note that the second iteration has wrongly placed some weight in sentence 2, which makes some intuitive sense, as sentence 2 is another place John had been.

- The process will iterate several times, hopefully at the final pass/iteration, the episodic memory (final GRU hints) contains all the information required to answer the question, these hints will be the input to the Answer module.

- Finally, the **Answer Module** generates an answer based on the episodic memory and question.
  The answer module could be implemented by another GRU or other dense module, trained with the cross-entropy error classification of the correct sequence, which can then be converted back to natural language.

Here are some good additional materials worth reading:

https://medium.com/@i_am_manish/unique-way-of-ai-chatbots-dynamic-memory-networks-nlp-5b7f7153d842

https://yerevann.github.io/2016/02/05/implementing-dynamic-memory-networks/

https://www.quora.com/What-are-dynamic-memory-networks

Enough theory, let's look at a DMN implementation.

1.5.3.2   DMN implementation source code

One DMN implementation using pytorch could be found at:

https://github.com/jhyuklee/dmn-pytorch

I modify it a little so that it can be run under pytorch 1.0, and put it at:

https://github.com/mingewang/dmn-pytorch/tree/comrite

I will not do code analysis for this code as:

- The code is not hard to understand once you grasp the DMN concepts.

- our focus is DMN+ network, I will do the code analysis there.

1.5.3.3   DMN implementation results

You can download the babi db from http://www.thespermwhale.com/jaseweston/babi/tasks_1-20_v1-2.tar.gz then unzip it, and place files in en-valid-10k under (home)/datasets/babi/en directory, also please place a pretrained GloVe under (home)/datasets/glove directory.

Now, let's run it:

```
1  (pytorch-gpu) $ python main.py
2  [nltk_data] Downloading package punkt to /home/mwang/nltk_data...
3  [nltk_data]   Package punkt is already up-to-date!
4  ### load dataset
5  ...
6
7  [QA set 1]
8  model parameters: 687,601
9
10  - Training Epoch 1
11    nn.utils.clip_grad_norm(m.parameters(), m.config.grad_max_norm)
12        [#####] 100.00% [1.82    0.00] time:  0: 0:38
13        total metrics:  1.82     0.00
14  - Validation
15        [#####] 100.00% [5.21    0.00] time:  0: 0: 1
16        total metrics:  5.21     0.00
17        best metrics:   0.00     0.00
18  - Testing
19        [#####] 100.00% [5.21    0.00] time:  0: 0: 1
20        total metrics:  5.21     0.00
21
22  ...
23  ...
24
25  - Training Epoch 16
26        [#####] 100.00% [1.78    21.37] time:  0: 0:37
27        total metrics:  1.78     21.37
28  - Validation
29        [#####] 100.00% [1.55    51.86] time:  0: 0: 1
30        total metrics:  1.55     51.86
31        => save checkpoint ./results/m1.pth
32        best metrics:   1.55     51.86
33  - Testing
```

```
34          [#####] 100.00% [1.55    52.73] time:   0: 0: 1
35          total metrics:   1.55     52.73
36
37  - Training Epoch 17
38          [#####] 100.00% [0.43    93.27] time:   0: 0:37
39          total metrics:   0.43     93.27
40  - Validation
41          [#####] 100.00% [0.06    100.00] time:   0: 0: 1
42          total metrics:   0.06     100.00
43          => save checkpoint ./results/m1.pth
44  - Load Validation/Testing
45          => load checkpoint ./results/m1.pth
46          [#####] 100.00% [0.06    100.00] time:   0: 0: 1
47          total metrics:   0.06     100.00
48          [#####] 100.00% [0.06    100.00] time:   0: 0: 1
49          total metrics:   0.06     100.00
50
51  ### end of experiment
```

The test results are 100%.

1.5.4 DMN+ (DMN plus) network

In 2016, Xiong et al. further applied these concepts to handle visual FAQ, and proposed DMN+ model.

It is a quite interesting work, see the figure below:

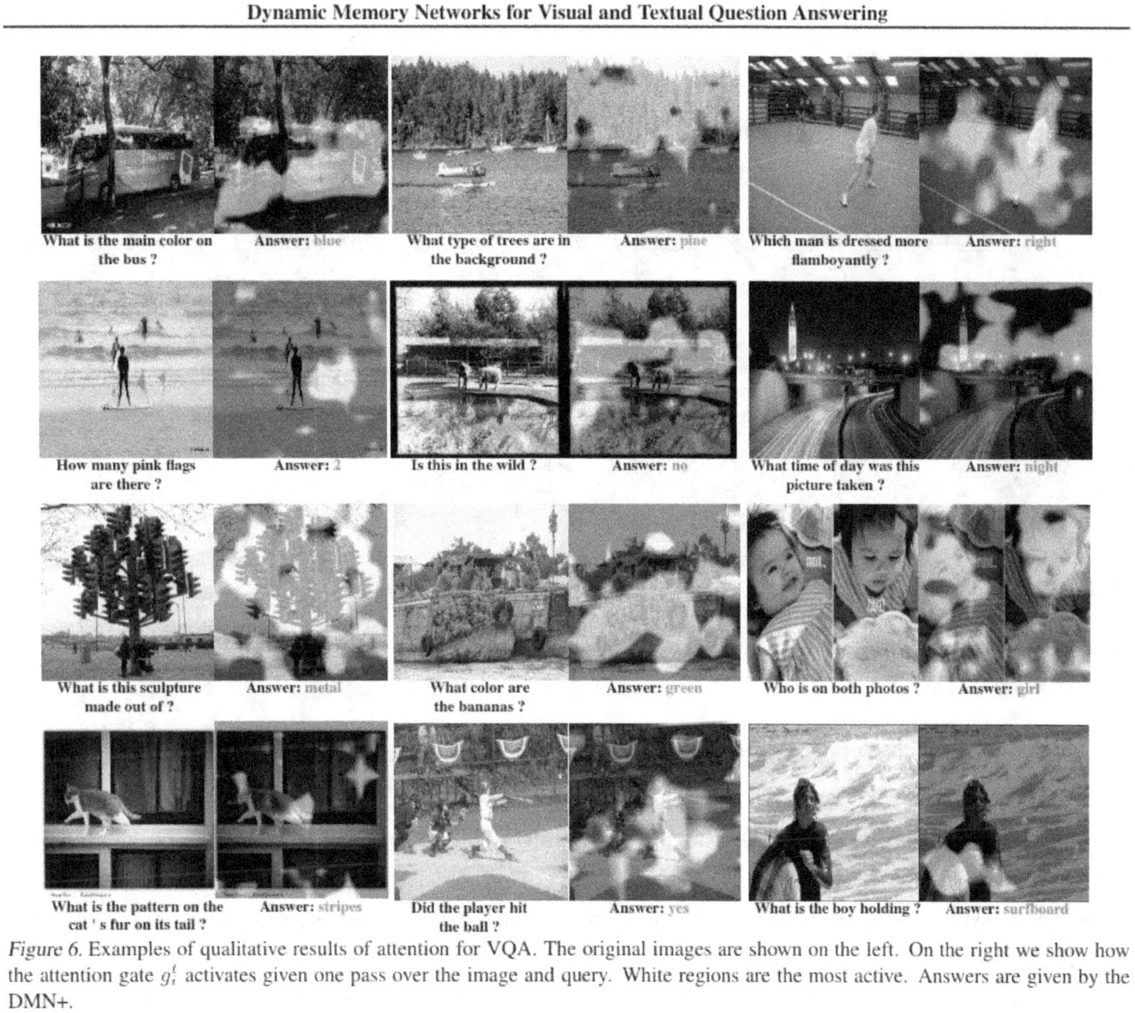
Dynamic Memory Networks for Visual and Textual Question Answering
What is the main color on the bus ?
Answer: blue
What type of trees are in the background ?
Answer: pine
Which man is dressed more flamboyantly ?
Answer: right
How many pink flags are there ?
Answer: 2
Is this in the wild ?
Answer: no
What time of day was this picture taken ?
Answer: night
What is this sculpture made out of ?
Answer: metal
What color are the bananas ?
Answer: green
Who is on both photos ?
Answer: girl
What is the pattern on the cat ' s fur on its tail ?
Answer: stripes
Did the player hit the ball ?
Answer: yes
What is the boy holding ?
Answer: surfboard
Figure 6. Examples of qualitative results of attention for VQA. The original images are shown on the left. On the right we show how the attention gate g_i^t activates given one pass over the image and query. White regions are the most active. Answers are given by the DMN+.

Figure 1.19: Dynamic Memory Network plus

Please see more details at: https://arxiv.org/pdf/1603.01417.pdf

This is a state-of-the-art memory network.

1.5.4.1 how DMN+ works

The main architecture remains the same as DMN.

The major differences from DMN are:

• A new input module is shown as following:

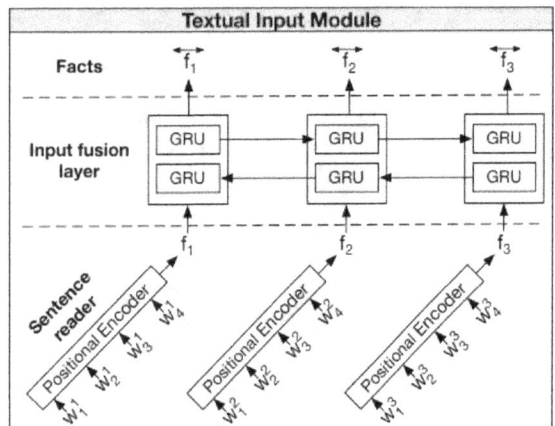
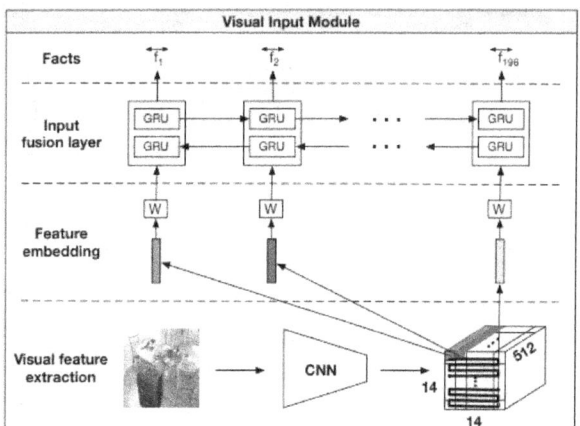

Figure 1.20: dmn+ input mode with fusion layer

The input module uses **Positional Encoder** and **BidirectionalGRU** to encode the input text representation in a much better way than DMN.

The intuition is a position of a word in a sentence matters, the positional encoder is just to keep/encode to some position information.

Also, the influence of a sentence in an article is not just one way (forward). So DMN+ adopts a bi-directional GRU in an input fusion layer, thus allows information from both past and future sentences to be used.

- New attention mechanism
  Instead of forcing attention score either 0 or 1 as in DMN, DMN+ uses an **Attention-based GRU** to calculate the attention.

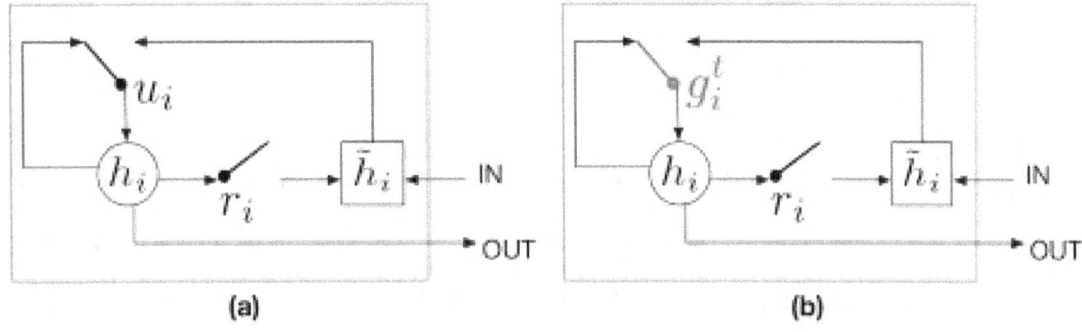

(a)   (b)

Figure 5. (a) The traditional GRU model, and (b) the proposed attention-based GRU model

Figure 1.21: dmn+ gru model

where g_i^t is a single scalar value, which can be calculated as:

$$z_i^t = [\overleftrightarrow{f_i} \circ q; \; \overleftrightarrow{f_i} \circ m^{t-1}; \; |\overleftrightarrow{f_i} - q|; \; |\overleftrightarrow{f_i} - m^{t-1}|] \quad (8)$$

$$Z_i^t = W^{(2)} \tanh\left(W^{(1)} z_i^t + b^{(1)}\right) + b^{(2)} \quad (9)$$

$$g_i^t = \frac{\exp(Z_i^t)}{\sum_{k=1}^{M_i} \exp(Z_k^t)} \quad (10)$$

where $\overleftrightarrow{f_i}$ is the ith fact, m^{t-1} is the previous episode memory, q is the original question, $\circ$ is the element-wise product, $|\cdot|$ is the element-wise absolute value, and ; represents concatenation of the vectors.

Figure 1.22: dmn+ attention gate math

Please take time to digest it, if you do not understand it please refer to the original paper for more details.

- Simplified the memory module update.
  It uses Attention-based GRU to compute the contextual vector representing the input relevant to previous memory state and the question, and finally uses this to update its next memory state.

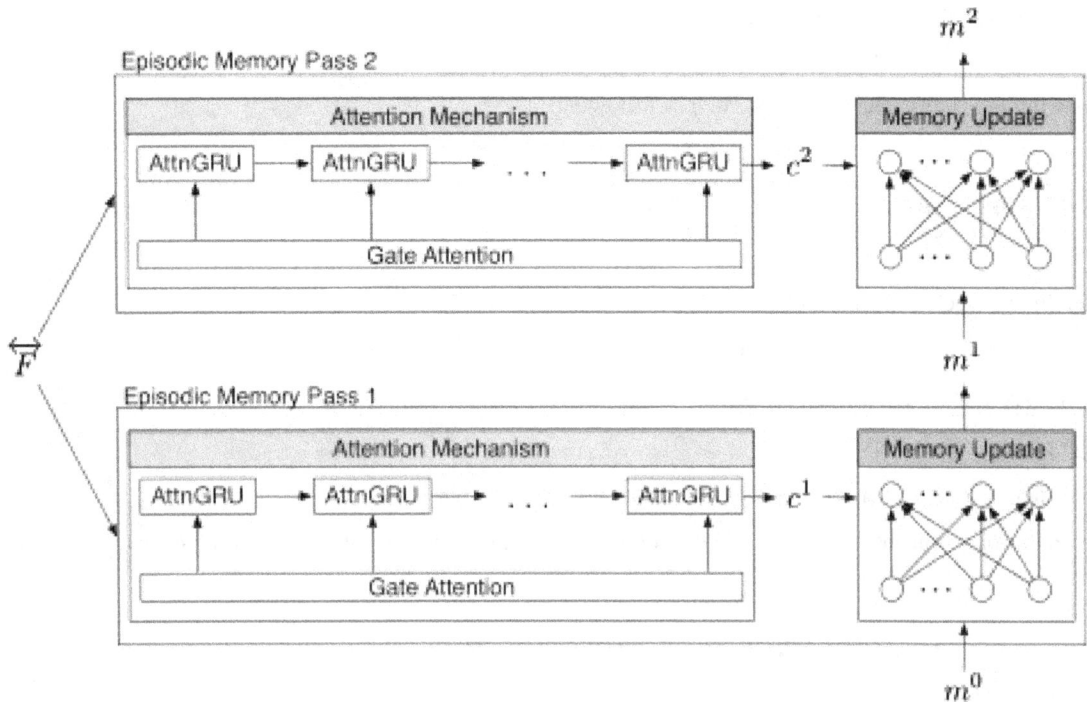

Figure 4. The episodic memory module of the DMN+ when using two passes. The $\overleftrightarrow{F}$ is the output of the input module.

Figure 1.23: dmn+ episodic memory

As shown in the figure above, the memory is updated using ReLU layer with input from previous **AttnGRU** and memory.

1.5.4.2 DMN+ source code analysis

There are several DMN+ plus implementations in github.

I found:

https://github.com/dandelin/Dynamic-memory-networks-plus-Pytorch

is relatively easy to follow.

I made some changes and updated to use pytorch 1.0 and cpu/gpu in the comrite branch.

https://github.com/mingewang/Dynamic-memory-networks-plus-Pytorch/

Please clone the repository and look at the code as following:

```
git clone https://github.com/mingewang/Dynamic-memory-networks-plus-Pytorch/
git checkout -b comrite origin/comrite
```

Or you can directly look at the code at:

https://github.com/mingewang/Dynamic-memory-networks-plus-Pytorch/tree/comrite

The main code is in those two files:

babi_loader.py, and babi_main.py.

The babi_loader.py load/convert/encode raw babi data into pytorch dataset.

For example, one question/answer of raw babi data (context, question, answer) will be converted/encoded as some number:

```
# raw context/question/answer
(Pdb) p unindexed[0]
{'C': ['Mary moved to the bathroom . ', 'John went to the hallway . '],
 'Q': 'Where is Mary', 'A': 'bathroom', 'S': [0]}
# will be encoded as:
(Pdb) p context[0]
[8, 3, 4, 5, 6, 7, 1]
(Pdb) p questions[0]
[11, 12, 2, 1]
(Pdb) p answers[0]
6
```

Most of the code in babi_loader.py is straightforward to understand.

One thing that needs to be noted is pad_collate around line 13. Why do we need that? By default, torch stacks the input image to form a tensor of size N*C*H*W, so every qa data in the batch must have the same shape. In order to load a batch with variable size input qa, we have to use our own **collate_fn**, which is used to pack a batch of qa data. In this case, it is pad_collate inside babi_loader.py.

Now let's look at the babi_main.py:

```python
from babi_loader import BabiDataset, pad_collate
import os
import torch
import torch.nn as nn
import torch.nn.functional as F
import torch.nn.init as init
from torch.autograd import Variable
from torch.utils.data import DataLoader

device = torch.device('cuda' if torch.cuda.is_available() else 'cpu')
print('Using device:', device)
print()

def position_encoding(embedded_sentence):
    '''
    embedded_sentence.size() -> (#batch, #sentence, #token, #embedding)
    l.size() -> (#sentence, #embedding)
    output.size() -> (#batch, #sentence, #embedding)
    '''
    _, _, slen, elen = embedded_sentence.size()

    l = [[(1 - s/(slen-1)) - (e/(elen-1)) * (1 - 2*s/(slen-1)) for e in range( ↩
        elen)] for s in range(slen)]
    l = torch.FloatTensor(l)
    l = l.unsqueeze(0) # for #batch
    l = l.unsqueeze(1) # for #sen
    l = l.expand_as(embedded_sentence)
    weighted = embedded_sentence * Variable(l.to(device))
    return torch.sum(weighted, dim=2).squeeze(2) # sum with tokens

class AttentionGRUCell(nn.Module):
    def __init__(self, input_size, hidden_size):
        super(AttentionGRUCell, self).__init__()
        self.hidden_size = hidden_size
        self.Wr = nn.Linear(input_size, hidden_size)
        init.xavier_normal_(self.Wr.state_dict()['weight'])
        self.Ur = nn.Linear(hidden_size, hidden_size)
```

```python
37              init.xavier_normal_(self.Ur.state_dict()['weight'])
38              self.W = nn.Linear(input_size, hidden_size)
39              init.xavier_normal_(self.W.state_dict()['weight'])
40              self.U = nn.Linear(hidden_size, hidden_size)
41              init.xavier_normal_(self.U.state_dict()['weight'])
42
43          def forward(self, fact, C, g):
44              '''
45              fact.size() -> (#batch, #hidden = #embedding)
46              c.size() -> (#hidden, ) -> (#batch, #hidden = #embedding)
47              r.size() -> (#batch, #hidden = #embedding)
48              h_tilda.size() -> (#batch, #hidden = #embedding)
49              g.size() -> (#batch, )
50              '''
51
52              r = torch.sigmoid(self.Wr(fact) + self.Ur(C))
53              h_tilda = torch.tanh(self.W(fact) + r * self.U(C))
54              g = g.unsqueeze(1).expand_as(h_tilda)
55              h = g * h_tilda + (1 - g) * C
56              return h
57
58  class AttentionGRU(nn.Module):
59      def __init__(self, input_size, hidden_size):
60          super(AttentionGRU, self).__init__()
61          self.hidden_size = hidden_size
62          self.AGRUCell = AttentionGRUCell(input_size, hidden_size)
63
64      def forward(self, facts, G):
65          '''
66          facts.size() -> (#batch, #sentence, #hidden = #embedding)
67          fact.size() -> (#batch, #hidden = #embedding)
68          G.size() -> (#batch, #sentence)
69          g.size() -> (#batch, )
70          C.size() -> (#batch, #hidden)
71          '''
72          batch_num, sen_num, embedding_size = facts.size()
73          C = Variable(torch.zeros(self.hidden_size)).to(device)
74          for sid in range(sen_num):
75              fact = facts[:, sid, :]
76              g = G[:, sid]
77              if sid == 0:
78                  C = C.unsqueeze(0).expand_as(fact)
```

```python
79              C = self.AGRUCell(fact, C, g)
80          return C
81
82  class EpisodicMemory(nn.Module):
83      def __init__(self, hidden_size):
84          super(EpisodicMemory, self).__init__()
85          self.AGRU = AttentionGRU(hidden_size, hidden_size)
86          self.z1 = nn.Linear(4 * hidden_size, hidden_size)
87          self.z2 = nn.Linear(hidden_size, 1)
88          self.next_mem = nn.Linear(3 * hidden_size, hidden_size)
89          init.xavier_normal_(self.z1.state_dict()['weight'])
90          init.xavier_normal_(self.z2.state_dict()['weight'])
91          init.xavier_normal_(self.next_mem.state_dict()['weight'])
92
93      def make_interaction(self, facts, questions, prevM):
94          '''
95          facts.size() -> (#batch, #sentence, #hidden = #embedding)
96          questions.size() -> (#batch, 1, #hidden)
97          prevM.size() -> (#batch, #sentence = 1, #hidden = #embedding)
98          z.size() -> (#batch, #sentence, 4 x #embedding)
99          G.size() -> (#batch, #sentence)
100          '''
101          batch_num, sen_num, embedding_size = facts.size()
102          questions = questions.expand_as(facts)
103          prevM = prevM.expand_as(facts)
104
105          z = torch.cat([
106              facts * questions,
107              facts * prevM,
108              torch.abs(facts - questions),
109              torch.abs(facts - prevM)
110          ], dim=2)
111
112          z = z.view(-1, 4 * embedding_size)
113
114          G = torch.tanh(self.z1(z))
115          G = self.z2(G)
116          G = G.view(batch_num, -1)
117          G = F.softmax(G, dim=1)
118
119          return G
120
```

```python
121     def forward(self, facts, questions, prevM):
122         '''
123         facts.size() -> (#batch, #sentence, #hidden = #embedding)
124         questions.size() -> (#batch, #sentence = 1, #hidden)
125         prevM.size() -> (#batch, #sentence = 1, #hidden = #embedding)
126         G.size() -> (#batch, #sentence)
127         C.size() -> (#batch, #hidden)
128         concat.size() -> (#batch, 3 x #embedding)
129         '''
130         G = self.make_interaction(facts, questions, prevM)
131         C = self.AGRU(facts, G)
132         concat = torch.cat([prevM.squeeze(1), C, questions.squeeze(1)], dim=1)
133         next_mem = F.relu(self.next_mem(concat))
134         next_mem = next_mem.unsqueeze(1)
135         return next_mem
136
137
138 class QuestionModule(nn.Module):
139     def __init__(self, vocab_size, hidden_size):
140         super(QuestionModule, self).__init__()
141         self.gru = nn.GRU(hidden_size, hidden_size, batch_first=True)
142
143     def forward(self, questions, word_embedding):
144         '''
145         questions.size() -> (#batch, #token)
146         word_embedding() -> (#batch, #token, #embedding)
147         gru() -> (1, #batch, #hidden)
148         '''
149         questions = word_embedding(questions)
150         _, questions = self.gru(questions)
151         questions = questions.transpose(0, 1)
152         return questions
153
154 class InputModule(nn.Module):
155     def __init__(self, vocab_size, hidden_size):
156         super(InputModule, self).__init__()
157         self.hidden_size = hidden_size
158         self.gru = nn.GRU(hidden_size, hidden_size, bidirectional=True,  ↵
                batch_first=True)
159         for name, param in self.gru.state_dict().items():
160             if 'weight' in name: init.xavier_normal_(param)
161         self.dropout = nn.Dropout(0.1)
```

```python
    def forward(self, contexts, word_embedding):
        '''
        contexts.size() -> (#batch, #sentence, #token)
        word_embedding() -> (#batch, #sentence x #token, #embedding)
        position_encoding() -> (#batch, #sentence, #embedding)
        facts.size() -> (#batch, #sentence, #hidden = #embedding)
        '''
        batch_num, sen_num, token_num = contexts.size()

        contexts = contexts.view(batch_num, -1)
        contexts = word_embedding(contexts)

        contexts = contexts.view(batch_num, sen_num, token_num, -1)
        contexts = position_encoding(contexts)
        contexts = self.dropout(contexts)

        h0 = Variable(torch.zeros(2, batch_num, self.hidden_size).to(device))
        facts, hdn = self.gru(contexts, h0)
        facts = facts[:, :, :hidden_size] + facts[:, :, hidden_size:]
        return facts

class AnswerModule(nn.Module):
    def __init__(self, vocab_size, hidden_size):
        super(AnswerModule, self).__init__()
        self.z = nn.Linear(2 * hidden_size, vocab_size)
        init.xavier_normal_(self.z.state_dict()['weight'])
        self.dropout = nn.Dropout(0.1)

    def forward(self, M, questions):
        M = self.dropout(M)
        concat = torch.cat([M, questions], dim=2).squeeze(1)
        z = self.z(concat)
        return z

class DMNPlus(nn.Module):
    def __init__(self, hidden_size, vocab_size, num_hop=3, qa=None):
        super(DMNPlus, self).__init__()
        self.num_hop = num_hop
        self.qa = qa
        self.word_embedding = nn.Embedding(vocab_size, hidden_size, padding_idx ↵
            =0, sparse=True).to(device)
```

```python
203            init.uniform_(self.word_embedding.state_dict()['weight'], a=-(3**0.5), b ↩
                   =3**0.5)
204        self.criterion = nn.CrossEntropyLoss(reduction='sum')
205
206        self.input_module = InputModule(vocab_size, hidden_size)
207        self.question_module = QuestionModule(vocab_size, hidden_size)
208        self.memory = EpisodicMemory(hidden_size)
209        self.answer_module = AnswerModule(vocab_size, hidden_size)
210
211    def forward(self, contexts, questions):
212        '''
213        contexts.size() -> (#batch, #sentence, #token) -> (#batch, #sentence, # ↩
                   hidden = #embedding)
214        questions.size() -> (#batch, #token) -> (#batch, 1, #hidden)
215        '''
216        facts = self.input_module(contexts, self.word_embedding)
217        questions = self.question_module(questions, self.word_embedding)
218        M = questions
219        for hop in range(self.num_hop):
220            M = self.memory(facts, questions, M)
221        preds = self.answer_module(M, questions)
222        return preds
223
224    def interpret_indexed_tensor(self, var):
225        if len(var.size()) == 3:
226            # var -> n x #sen x #token
227            for n, sentences in enumerate(var):
228                for i, sentence in enumerate(sentences):
229                    s = ' '.join([self.qa.IVOCAB[elem.data[0]] for elem in ↩
                           sentence])
230                    print(f'{n}th of batch, {i}th sentence, {s}')
231        elif len(var.size()) == 2:
232            # var -> n x #token
233            for n, sentence in enumerate(var):
234                s = ' '.join([self.qa.IVOCAB[elem.data[0]] for elem in sentence])
235                print(f'{n}th of batch, {s}')
236        elif len(var.size()) == 1:
237            # var -> n (one token per batch)
238            for n, token in enumerate(var):
239                s = self.qa.IVOCAB[token.data[0]]
240                print(f'{n}th of batch, {s}')
241
```

```python
242     def get_loss(self, contexts, questions, targets):
243         output = self.forward(contexts, questions)
244         loss = self.criterion(output, targets)
245         reg_loss = 0
246         for param in self.parameters():
247             reg_loss += 0.001 * torch.sum(param * param)
248         preds = F.softmax(output, dim=1)
249         _, pred_ids = torch.max(preds, dim=1)
250         corrects = (pred_ids.data == answers.data)
251         acc = torch.mean(corrects.float())
252         return loss + reg_loss, acc
253
254 if __name__ == '__main__':
255     for run in range(10):
256         for task_id in range(1, 21):
257             dset = BabiDataset(task_id)
258             vocab_size = len(dset.QA.VOCAB)
259             hidden_size = 80
260
261             model = DMNPlus(hidden_size, vocab_size, num_hop=3, qa=dset.QA)
262             model.to(device)
263             early_stopping_cnt = 0
264             early_stopping_flag = False
265             best_acc = 0
266             optim = torch.optim.Adam(model.parameters())
267
268
269             for epoch in range(256):
270                 dset.set_mode('train')
271                 train_loader = DataLoader(
272                     dset, batch_size=100, shuffle=True, collate_fn=pad_collate
273                 )
274
275                 model.train()
276                 if not early_stopping_flag:
277                     total_acc = 0
278                     cnt = 0
279                     for batch_idx, data in enumerate(train_loader):
280                         optim.zero_grad()
281                         contexts, questions, answers = data
282                         batch_size = contexts.size()[0]
283                         contexts = Variable(contexts.long().to(device))
```

```
284            questions = Variable(questions.long().to(device))
285            answers = Variable(answers.to(device))
286
287            loss, acc = model.get_loss(contexts, questions, answers)
288            loss.backward()
289            total_acc += acc * batch_size
290            cnt += batch_size
291
292            if batch_idx % 20 == 0:
293                print(f'[Task {task_id}, Epoch {epoch}] [Training] ↩
                        loss : {loss.data.item(): {10}.{8}}, acc : { ↩
                        total_acc / cnt  : {5}.{4}}, batch_idx : { ↩
                        batch_idx}')
294            optim.step()
295
296        dset.set_mode('valid')
297        valid_loader = DataLoader(
298            dset, batch_size=100, shuffle=False, collate_fn= ↩
                pad_collate
299        )
300
301        model.eval()
302        total_acc = 0
303        cnt = 0
304        for batch_idx, data in enumerate(valid_loader):
305            contexts, questions, answers = data
306            batch_size = contexts.size()[0]
307            contexts = Variable(contexts.long().to(device))
308            questions = Variable(questions.long().to(device))
309            answers = Variable(answers.to(device))
310
311            _, acc = model.get_loss(contexts, questions, answers)
312            total_acc += acc * batch_size
313            cnt += batch_size
314
315        total_acc = total_acc / cnt
316        if total_acc > best_acc:
317            best_acc = total_acc
318            best_state = model.state_dict()
319            early_stopping_cnt = 0
320        else:
321            early_stopping_cnt += 1
```

```
322            if early_stopping_cnt > 20:
323                early_stopping_flag = True
324
325        print(f'[Run {run}, Task {task_id}, Epoch {epoch}] [Validate] ↩
               Accuracy : {total_acc: {5}.{4}}')
326        with open('log.txt', 'a') as fp:
327            fp.write(f'[Run {run}, Task {task_id}, Epoch {epoch}] [ ↩
                   Validate] Accuracy : {total_acc: {5}.{4}}' + '\n')
328        if total_acc == 1.0:
329            break
330    else:
331        print(f'[Run {run}, Task {task_id}] Early Stopping at Epoch { ↩
               epoch}, Valid Accuracy : {best_acc: {5}.{4}}')
332        break
333
334    dset.set_mode('test')
335    test_loader = DataLoader(
336        dset, batch_size=100, shuffle=False, collate_fn=pad_collate
337    )
338    test_acc = 0
339    cnt = 0
340
341    for batch_idx, data in enumerate(test_loader):
342        contexts, questions, answers = data
343        batch_size = contexts.size()[0]
344        contexts = Variable(contexts.long().to(device))
345        questions = Variable(questions.long().to(device))
346        answers = Variable(answers.to(device))
347
348        model.load_state_dict(best_state)
349        _, acc = model.get_loss(contexts, questions, answers)
350        test_acc += acc * batch_size
351        cnt += batch_size
352    print(f'[Run {run}, Task {task_id}, Epoch {epoch}] [Test] Accuracy :  ↩
           {test_acc / cnt: {5}.{4}}')
353    os.makedirs('models', exist_ok=True)
354    with open(f'models/task{task_id}_epoch{epoch}_run{run}_acc{test_acc/ ↩
           cnt}.pth', 'wb') as fp:
355        torch.save(model.state_dict(), fp)
356    with open('log.txt', 'a') as fp:
357        fp.write(f'[Run {run}, Task {task_id}, Epoch {epoch}] [Test] ↩
               Accuracy : {total_acc: {5}.{4}}' + '\n')
```

- Line 14 - 28 specify how we do the position encoding.
  Line 22 is the magic encoding formula according to the DMN+ paper. The main point is: it encodes some position information, which will be multiplied with the original embedded_sentence as in Line 27.

- Line 30 - 55 defines the AttentionGRUCell.
  Most of the code is just a normal GRU implementation using a linear layer. One difference from normal GRU is Line 55, we use g (passed in as we said earlier in Figure 10.12), instead of u, to calculate hint. For comparison, I put the normal GRU formula here:

$$u_i = \sigma\left(W^{(u)}x_i + U^{(u)}h_{i-1} + b^{(u)}\right) \qquad (1)$$

$$r_i = \sigma\left(W^{(r)}x_i + U^{(r)}h_{i-1} + b^{(r)}\right) \qquad (2)$$

$$\tilde{h}_i = \tanh\left(Wx_i + r_i \circ Uh_{i-1} + b^{(h)}\right) \qquad (3)$$

$$h_i = u_i \circ \tilde{h}_i + (1 - u_i) \circ h_{i-1} \qquad (4)$$

where σ is the sigmoid activation function, $\circ$ is an element-wise product, $W^{(z)}, W^{(r)}, W \in \mathbb{R}^{n_H \times n_I}, U^{(z)}, U^{(r)}, U \in \mathbb{R}^{n_H \times n_H}$, n_H is the hidden size, and n_I is the input size.

Figure 1.24: normal GRU calculation

AttentionGRUCell calculates a hint based on (one) fact, previous hint/context and soft attention g.

- Line 58 - 80, defines an AttentionGRU.
  It basically updates the hidden state using AttentionGRUCell defined before by iterating over all the sentences. The final hidden state is called the contextual vector, which is used to update the next memory state.

- Line 82 - 135 defines the episodic memory module.
  It retrieves information from the final input facts by focusing attention on a subset of these facts using gate values.

- Line 93 - 119 is to calculate the soft attention according to Figure 10.12.
  The 4*embedding_size in Line 112 is because previously z concatenate 4 items into one.

- Line 121 - 134 defines how to update episodic memory.
  First, we calculate G as defined before, then we pass G to AttnGRU to get context information, finally, we use Relu to update new memory as shown in Figure 10.13.

- Line 138 - 152 defines question module.
  It basically just does the word_embedding for the question first, then apply GRU on it.

- Line 154 - 182 defines the input module. In Line 176 we do the position encoding, then pass it to a bi-directional GRU. Line 181 basically concatenate forward/backward GRU output together according to:

$$\overrightarrow{f_i} = GRU_{fwd}(f_i, \overrightarrow{f_{i-1}}) \tag{5}$$

$$\overleftarrow{f_i} = GRU_{bwd}(f_i, \overleftarrow{f_{i+1}}) \tag{6}$$

$$\overleftrightarrow{f_i} = \overleftarrow{f_i} + \overrightarrow{f_i} \tag{7}$$

where f_i is the input fact at timestep i, $\overrightarrow{f_i}$ is the hidden state of the forward GRU at timestep i, and $\overleftarrow{f_i}$ is the hidden state of the backward GRU at timestep i. This allows contextual information from both future and past facts to impact $\overleftrightarrow{f_i}$.

Figure 1.25: input using bi-directional GRU

- Line 184 - 195 defines the answer module.
  It basically looks up an answer from memory as shown in line 193-194.

- Line 197 - 253 defines DMNPlus module.
  It glues all the previous modules together.

The rest of the code is a pretty standard pytorch training code.

I hope, with my explanation, you can understand the code without much difficulties.

1.5.4.3 DMN+ runing results

Now, let's run it.

```
(pytorch_env) $  chmod +x fetch_data.sh
(pytorch_env) $  ./fetch_data.sh

(pytorch_env) Dynamic-memory-networks-plus-Pytorch$ python babi_main.py
Using device: cpu

[Task 1, Epoch 0] [Training] loss :  294.96686, acc :  0.13, batch_idx : 0
[Task 1, Epoch 0] [Training] loss :  181.05008, acc :  0.1733, batch_idx : 20
[Task 1, Epoch 0] [Training] loss :  181.95341, acc :  0.1878, batch_idx : 40
[Task 1, Epoch 0] [Training] loss :  174.61531, acc :  0.207, batch_idx : 60
[Task 1, Epoch 0] [Training] loss :  161.29692, acc :  0.2559, batch_idx : 80
[Run 0, Task 1, Epoch 0] [Validate] Accuracy :  0.538
[Task 1, Epoch 1] [Training] loss :  159.31825, acc :  0.42, batch_idx : 0
[Task 1, Epoch 1] [Training] loss :  120.42671, acc :  0.4981, batch_idx : 20
[Task 1, Epoch 1] [Training] loss :  128.74518, acc :  0.5056, batch_idx : 40
[Task 1, Epoch 1] [Training] loss :   84.89447, acc :  0.5461, batch_idx : 60
[Task 1, Epoch 1] [Training] loss :  15.190652, acc :  0.6298, batch_idx : 80
[Run 0, Task 1, Epoch 1] [Validate] Accuracy :  0.998
[Task 1, Epoch 2] [Training] loss :  7.4424944, acc :  0.99, batch_idx : 0
[Task 1, Epoch 2] [Training] loss :  3.8703742, acc :  0.9919, batch_idx : 20
[Task 1, Epoch 2] [Training] loss :  4.3218408, acc :  0.991, batch_idx : 40
[Task 1, Epoch 2] [Training] loss :  3.3983481, acc :  0.9921, batch_idx : 60
[Task 1, Epoch 2] [Training] loss :  3.3103867, acc :  0.9937, batch_idx : 80
[Run 0, Task 1, Epoch 2] [Validate] Accuracy :   1.0
[Run 0, Task 1, Epoch 2] [Test] Accuracy :   1.0
```

```
27   [Task 2, Epoch 0] [Training] loss :    361.591, acc :    0.0, batch_idx : 0
28   [Task 2, Epoch 0] [Training] loss :    195.4364, acc :    0.1657, batch_idx : 20
29   [Task 2, Epoch 0] [Training] loss :    187.645, acc :    0.168, batch_idx : 40
30   [Task 2, Epoch 0] [Training] loss :    191.41089, acc :    0.1685, batch_idx : 60
31   [Task 2, Epoch 0] [Training] loss :    190.03619, acc :    0.1702, batch_idx : 80
32   [Run 0, Task 2, Epoch 0] [Validate] Accuracy :    0.177
33   [Task 2, Epoch 1] [Training] loss :    183.7915, acc :    0.22, batch_idx : 0
34   ...
35   ...
```

The result is pretty good.

1.5.4.4   DMN+ applications

The DMM+ can not only be applied to regular question answering (QA) in NLP such as Babi QA, but also be extended to handle visual question answering (VQA) etc.

Considering DMN+ can answer questions without providing supporting facts, it could probably be applied to many other applications.

1.6   summary

In this chapter, we introduced several important techniques to handle text, language-related NLP tasks.

In particular, you should:

- know how to use pre-trained word embedding and how to train your own word embedding.

- understand how seq2seq model is applied to language translation, chatbot.
  Hopefully, you are able to apply seq2seq to new tasks.

- understand how DMN/DMN+ network works.
  Advanced readers may be able to apply DMN+ to some interesting projects.

Chapter 2

Optical character recognition

Quote from Wikipedia:

```
Optical character recognition (also optical character reader, OCR
is the mechanical or electronic conversion of images of typed,
handwritten or printed text into machine-encoded text,
whether from a scanned document, a photo of a document,
a scene-photo (for example the text on signs
and billboards in a landscape photo)
or from subtitle text superimposed on an image
(for example from a television broadcast).
```

OCR has lots of applications, for example: scan then digitize invoice, bank statement, receipts, business card , etc.

Traditionally, OCR systems were heavily pipelined with many hand-built and highly tuned modules, which assume all kinds of conditions/presumptions.

The last few years have seen deep learning being successfully applied to OCR, thus enable us to design a new generation of OCR without crafting manually-designed/complex modules.

The new generation of OCR could be split into two steps:

- First, we can use regular computer vision techniques to take an image of a document and segment it into either lines or words. We can call it the word detector or line detector.

- Then, we feed each word or a line into a DNN, which will turn the word/line image into actual texts.

There is already a pretty good open source OCR software at:

https://github.com/tesseract-ocr/tesseract

Actually, tesseract 4 added a **LSTM based OCR engine** that delivers significantly higher accuracy (on document images) than the previous versions, but at the expense of requiring significantly more training data and training time compared to the previous base Tesseract.

According to:

https://github.com/tesseract-ocr/tesseract/wiki/TrainingTesseract-4.00

Tesseract 4.00 has been trained on about 400000 textlines spanning about 4500 fonts. The training time could take a few days to a couple of weeks to just give you some idea of how long the training could take.

In this chapter, we will not focus on Tesseract, but, instead, we will use a simplified OCR example to illustrate how we could apply deep learning to OCR, at the same time, learn a pretty useful technique called **Connectionist temporal classification (CTC)**.

2.1 OCR line detector or word detector

As outlined before, the first step of OCR is normally to split an image to either lines or some words using some computer vision techniques.

The following python example showed how to split lines on an image using OpenCV (https://opencv.org/), a famous computer vision open source project.

The code (with some minor changes) was copied from:

https://stackoverflow.com/questions/34981144/split-text-lines-in-scanned-document

The credits should go to those authors.

```
1  #!/usr/bin/python
2  # copied from:
3  # https://stackoverflow.com/questions/34981144/split-text-lines-in-scanned- ↩
       document
4  # with some minor changes
5  # you may need to install opencv and its python libs
6  # apt-get install opencv-python
7
```

```
 8  import cv2
 9  import numpy as np
10
11  ## (1) read
12  img = cv2.imread("ocr_test.png")
13  gray = cv2.cvtColor(img, cv2.COLOR_BGR2GRAY)
14
15  ## (2) threshold
16  th, threshed = cv2.threshold(gray, 127, 255, cv2.THRESH_BINARY_INV|cv2. ←
        THRESH_OTSU)
17
18  ## (3) minAreaRect on the nozeros
19  pts = cv2.findNonZero(threshed)
20  ret = cv2.minAreaRect(pts)
21
22  (cx,cy), (w,h), ang = ret
23  if w>h:
24      w,h = h,w
25      ang += 90
26
27  ## (4) Find rotated matrix, do rotation.
28  M = cv2.getRotationMatrix2D((cx,cy), ang, 1.0)
29  rotated = cv2.warpAffine(threshed, M, (img.shape[1], img.shape[0]))
30
31  ## (5) find and draw the upper and lower boundary of each lines
32  # for python3
33  #hist = cv2.reduce(rotated,1, cv2.cv.REDUCE_AVG).reshape(-1)
34  # for python2
35  hist = cv2.reduce(rotated,1, cv2.cv.CV_REDUCE_AVG).reshape(-1)
36
37  th = 2
38  H,W = img.shape[:2]
39  uppers = [y for y in range(H-1) if hist[y]<=th and hist[y+1]>th]
40  lowers = [y for y in range(H-1) if hist[y]>th and hist[y+1]<=th]
41
42  rotated2 = cv2.cvtColor(rotated, cv2.COLOR_GRAY2BGR)
43  for y in uppers:
44      cv2.line(rotated2, (0,y), (W, y), (255,0,0), 1)
45      print("uppers y is:", y )
46
47  for y in lowers:
48      cv2.line(rotated2, (0,y), (W, y), (0,255,0), 1)
```

```
49      print("lowers y is:", y )
50
51  cv2.imwrite("result.png", rotated2)
52
53  # write file line by line
54  i = 0
55  for ty in uppers:
56    found_top = False
57    for ly in lowers:
58      if found_top == False and ly > ty:
59        found_top = True
60        print("ly is:", ly )
61        print("ty is:", ty )
62        # revert black/write for our ocr format
63        roi = cv2.bitwise_not( rotated[ty-2:ly+2, 0:W] )
64        cv2.imwrite('line_{}.png'.format(i), roi)
65        i = i+1
```

The basic idea here is to find minAreaRect using opencv, then find and draw upper and lower bounds of lines.

It seems work well, here is my testing input image:

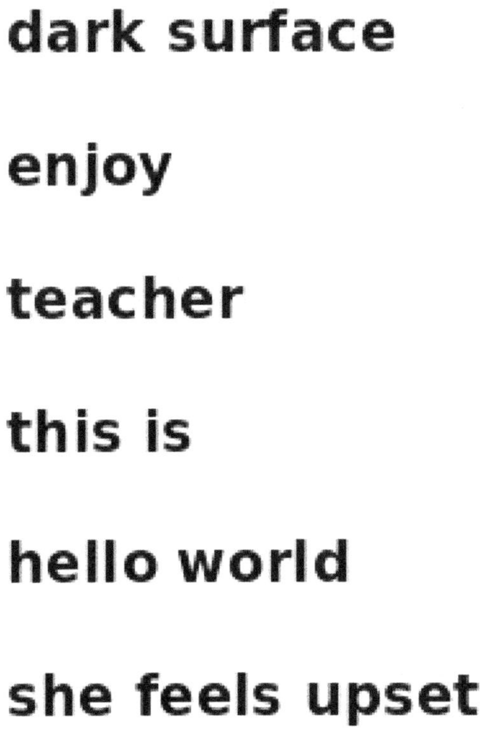

dark surface

enjoy

teacher

this is

hello world

she feels upset

Figure 2.1: ocr_test image

And it was split into several lines (I just showed two here):

dark surface

Figure 2.2: first line

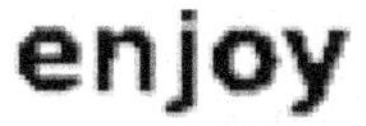

enjoy

Figure 2.3: second line

2.2 OCR with CTC

With an image split into lines, our second step is to do the real OCR on those lines.

How can we achieve that?

Since it is related to images, some CNN layers could be used to extract image features. Also, the final output is some sort of sequence, so RNN layers could be used.

Naively, we can feed an image into CNN, if we knew a character/word boundary in the image, we could reshape the CNN data into some sort of (time-step) sequences, which are then fed into RNN layers, the last RNN layer can predict character/text at each time step, right?

Remember, RNNs can only be trained to make a series of independent label classifications. For example, it can not predict half character "a" or half word. This means that the training data must be pre-segmented as words or characters.

So we need to:

- know how to reshape correctly at character/word boundary, which sounds impossible.

- or annotate the training data-set at character-level/word level, then we find some way to feed this into the network, which is quite time-consuming.

In 2006, Alex, etc proposed a novel method called connectionist temporal classification (CTC) to tackle this problem. (https://www.cs.toronto.edu/~graves/icml_2006.pdf)

CTC removed the need for pre-segmented training data and post-processed outputs. **The basic idea is to interpret the network outputs as a probability distribution over all possible label sequences, conditioned on a given input sequence. Given this distribution, an objective function can be derived that directly maximizes the probabilities of the correct labelings**.

It is a quite useful tool for applications like: OCR, voice recognition, etc. For example, the famous Baidu's deepspeech utilized CTC for its speech-to-text.

The main advantage of CTC is: **detecting word boundary or voice/word boundary is not needed, CTC will train the network to do so**.

Sounds magic? Let's learn CTC in the next section.

2.2.1 Connectionist temporal classification (CTC)

Here is how CTC works at a very high level:

- The CTC works on a sequence of data.
  For example, it works a sequence of text, instead of the character/word level.

- at the first step, we split speech signals or an OCR test image into **many very small time-steps** or areas for images. Obviously some time-step/area may be in the middle of an object in the image. That is the beauty of CTC, it do not need to know the boundary of the object (word, character, or any object etc).

- at the second step, we try to detect/recognize each time-step/area as either a valid letter or a blank character. The is the another key point of CTC. More accurately, **the network will output the probability distribute at each time-step.**

- Finally, we try to find a path with the maximum probability of correct labelings.

We will dig into CTC with more details in the following sections.

2.2.1.1 CTC blank token

One key concept CTC introduced is a new token called the **blank token**, which enables us to calculate the probabilities at each time-step and the probability of an whole output sequence naturally. The example below will show that clearly.

Let's denote the blank toke here as: -,
just for the sake of easy reading, please do not confuse with a real - .

For example, for a given text image: "hello" (remember it is an image)

CTC can use the following encoding combination to represent hello:

```
output                 CTC reduced results
at each time step
h--ee-ll-l-o           ---> hello

h---e-ll-lo-           ---> hello

hh--e-ll-lo-           ---> hello

...
```

The rule is: we can insert arbitrary many blanks at any position, which will be removed when decoding it. But we must insert a blank between duplicate characters like in "hello". Furthermore, we can repeat each character as often as we like.

If the output is the following, CTC will not reduce/decode it as hello:

```
1  output          CTC reduced results
2
3  h-h-e-l--lo-  ---> hhello
4
5  hh--e-ll--o-  ---> helo
```

You may ask how long/how wide should a time-step be, so that it could serve as a blank token?

Well, it depends on the problem domain. For example, for a regular OCR, we may choose 1pt, as any written symbol should be wider than that.

2.2.1.2 CTC probability path/graph

An NN using CTC normally uses a softmax dense layer to output a probability distribution over its output tokens space for each time-step.

For example: let our output tokens set to be: [a, b, -], and output 3 time steps. The output will look like:

Table 2.1: ctc output tables

	t0	t1	t2
a	0.4	0.5	0.3
b	0	0.2	0.6
-	0.6	0.3	0.1

For each time-step, the total probability will be 1.

The number of possible sequences (at time-step level) is: (output token size)$^{(number\_of\_time\_steps)}$

In this case, it is: $(3)^3 = 27$.

For example:

```
1  one possible path is: aa-, the probability is:  0.4 * 0.5 * 0.1 = 0.02
2  another one is:       a-a, the probability is : 0.4 * 0.3 * 0.3 = 0.036
3  the third one is:     -aa, the probability is : 0.6 * 0.5 * 0.3 = 0.09
4  another possible is:  aaa, the probability is :  0.4 * 0.5 * 0.3 = 0.06
5                        ...
6                   ..   ab-  ...
7                   ..   abb  ...
8   ..
```

As you can see, the first three actually will generate the same output sequence according to our rule, so for this sequence: aa, we need to sum all those probabilities together, thus:

```
1  p(aa) =  p(aa-) + p(a-a) + p(-aa)
2        =  0.02 + 0.036 + 0.09
3        =  0.146
```

In order to calculate the probabilities distribution, the same procedure will be applied to other valid sequences.

The CTC is an efficient way to calculate the probability distribution and deduce the loss against ground true.

The gory details of math are skipped, but you get the idea.

Interesting readers can found more details at:

https://distill.pub/2017/ctc/

2.2.1.3 CTC decoding

Assuming we have a trained CTC network, now, we input one new image/sequence data, it outputs something like the previous table.

We need to decode what was the input sequence.

One naïve way to decode is:

- pick the most likely token at each time-step

- reduce it to a sequence according to CTC rule.

That is called **best path decoding or greedy decoding**.

In the previous example, the output was: (I intentionally reproduced the table here for easy reading)

Table 2.2: ctc output tables

	t0	t1	t2
a	0.4	0.5	0.3
b	0	0.2	0.6
-	0.6	0.3	0.1

```
1  So at that t0 step, we will choose: -    ( as 0.6 is the largest )
2            t1 step, we will choose: a    ( as 0.5 is the largest )
3            t2 step, we will choose: b    ( as 0.6 is the largest )
```

Thus, the whole output sequence we picked using the best path decoding will be: -ab, and according to CTC rule, we will decode it as: ab

Other decoding algorithms, such as **bean search**, will give better results, of course, at the expense of computing power.

The description from Wikipedia regarding the bean search should give you enough information to understand use of pytorch bean search API:

```
1  Beam search uses breadth-first search to build its search tree.
2  At each level of the tree, it generates all successors of the states at the    ↵
       current level,
3  sorting them in increasing order of heuristic cost.
4
5  However, it only stores a predetermined number, beta ,
6  of best states at each level (called the beam width).
7  Only those states are expanded next.
```

Again, I skipped the gory details of how it is used in CTC. Interesting readers can read more details at:
https://distill.pub/2017/ctc/

 Warning
Either best path decoding or bean search can NOT be guaranteed to output the most likely sequence.

Fortunately, pytorch has already done those heavy-lift jobs for us, it has implemented CTC loss and decoding algorithms in its library. We just need to know how to use it.

In the next section, we will look at an OCR example, show you how CTC and its associated pytorch API get used there.

2.2.2   Convolutional Recurrent Neural Network for OCR

A popular model to do the OCR is: **Convolutional Recurrent Neural Network CRNN**. See the original paper at: https://arxiv.org/pdf/1507.05717v1.pdf

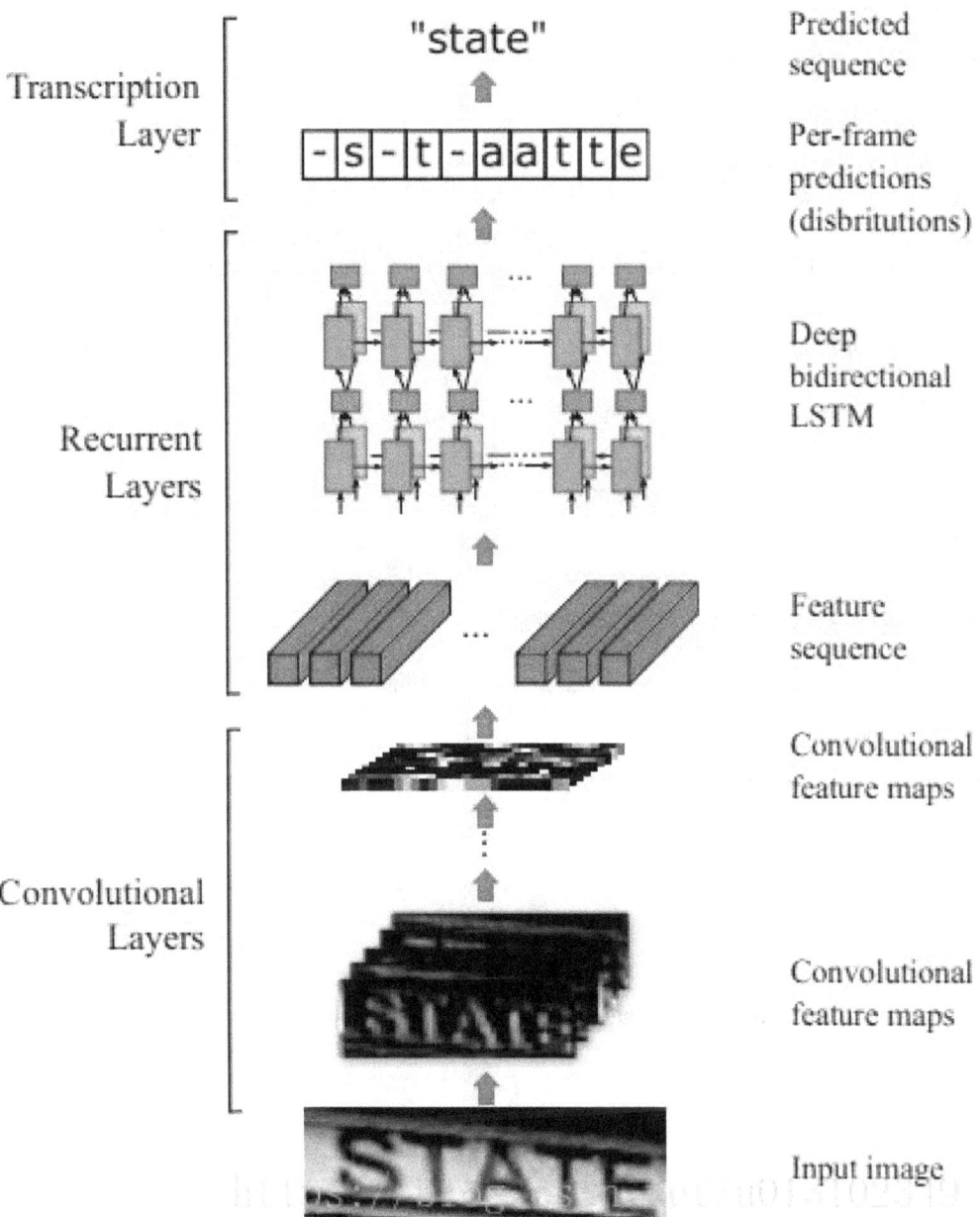

Figure 2.4: CRNN architecture

As shown in the figure above, CRNN works as the following:

- the image data will be fed to CNN layers first,

- then reshaped to feed into RNN layers,

- finally output to a software dense layer with CTC loss.

- We will train the model end-to-end to recognize sequence-like objects in images.

Recall we applied RNN to MNIST images data directly in the previous RNN chapter, the CRNN model used here is similar to that model. The difference is we added a convolutional layer that extracts image feature in the front-end, and CTCLoss is used at the end.

The main advantage of this model is:

- It can be trained directly from sequence labels (for instance, words/text) requiring no detailed annotations (for instance, characters, space).

- It is unconstrained to the lengths of sequence-like objects, requiring only height normalization in both training and testing phases.

2.2.3   pytorch crnn example and code analysis

A relative simple/easy-to-understand crnn implementation can be found at:

https://github.com/jingjing-you/CRNN_OCR.pytorch

I updated to pytorch 1.0, and put it into a comrite branch.

https://github.com/mingewang/CRNN_OCR.pytorch

You can read the code at:

https://github.com/mingewang/CRNN_OCR.pytorch/tree/comrite

Most of the code is easy to understand.

The CRNN.py defines a CRNN model, and dataloader.py defines a dataset. The train.py defines how to train the model.

Table 1. Network configuration summary. The first row is the top layer. 'k', 's' and 'p' stand for kernel size, stride and padding size respectively

Type	Configurations
Transcription	-
Bidirectional-LSTM	#hidden units:256
Bidirectional-LSTM	#hidden units:256
Map-to-Sequence	-
Convolution	#maps:512, k:2 $\times$ 2, s:1, p:0
MaxPooling	Window:1 $\times$ 2, s:2
BatchNormalization	-
Convolution	#maps:512, k:3 $\times$ 3, s:1, p:1
BatchNormalization	-
Convolution	#maps:512, k:3 $\times$ 3, s:1, p:1
MaxPooling	Window:1 $\times$ 2, s:2
Convolution	#maps:256, k:3 $\times$ 3, s:1, p:1
Convolution	#maps:256, k:3 $\times$ 3, s:1, p:1
MaxPooling	Window:2 $\times$ 2, s:2
Convolution	#maps:128, k:3 $\times$ 3, s:1, p:1
MaxPooling	Window:2 $\times$ 2, s:2
Convolution	#maps:64, k:3 $\times$ 3, s:1, p:1
Input	$W \times 32$ gray-scale image

Figure 2.5: CRNN network parameters

The figure above and code below is the model's parameters, and input/output shape:

```
1  (pytorch_env) $ python CRNN.py
2  CRNN(
3    (cnn): Sequential(
4      (conv0): Conv2d(1, 64, kernel_size=(3, 3), stride=(1, 1), padding=(1, 1))
5      (relu0): ReLU(inplace)
6      (pooling0): MaxPool2d(kernel_size=2, stride=2, padding=0, dilation=1, ↩
          ceil_mode=False)
7      (conv1): Conv2d(64, 128, kernel_size=(3, 3), stride=(1, 1), padding=(1, 1))
8      (relu1): ReLU(inplace)
9      (pooling1): MaxPool2d(kernel_size=2, stride=2, padding=0, dilation=1, ↩
          ceil_mode=False)
10     (conv2): Conv2d(128, 256, kernel_size=(3, 3), stride=(1, 1), padding=(1, 1))
11     (batchnorm2): BatchNorm2d(256, eps=1e-05, momentum=0.1, affine=True, ↩
          track_running_stats=True)
12     (relu2): ReLU(inplace)
13     (conv3): Conv2d(256, 256, kernel_size=(3, 3), stride=(1, 1), padding=(1, 1))
14     (relu3): ReLU(inplace)
15     (pooling2): MaxPool2d(kernel_size=(2, 2), stride=(2, 1), padding=(0, 1), ↩
          dilation=1, ceil_mode=False)
16     (conv4): Conv2d(256, 512, kernel_size=(3, 3), stride=(1, 1), padding=(1, 1))
17     (batchnorm4): BatchNorm2d(512, eps=1e-05, momentum=0.1, affine=True, ↩
          track_running_stats=True)
18     (relu4): ReLU(inplace)
19     (conv5): Conv2d(512, 512, kernel_size=(3, 3), stride=(1, 1), padding=(1, 1))
20     (relu5): ReLU(inplace)
21     (pooling3): MaxPool2d(kernel_size=(2, 2), stride=(2, 1), padding=(0, 1), ↩
          dilation=1, ceil_mode=False)
22     (conv6): Conv2d(512, 512, kernel_size=(2, 2), stride=(1, 1))
23     (batchnorm6): BatchNorm2d(512, eps=1e-05, momentum=0.1, affine=True, ↩
          track_running_stats=True)
24     (relu6): ReLU(inplace)
25   )
26   (rnn): Sequential(
27     (0): BidirectionalLSTM(
28       (rnn): LSTM(512, 256, bidirectional=True)
29       (embedding): Linear(in_features=512, out_features=256, bias=True)
30     )
31     (1): BidirectionalLSTM(
32       (rnn): LSTM(256, 256, bidirectional=True)
33       (embedding): Linear(in_features=512, out_features=37, bias=True)
34     )
```

```
35      )
36  )
37
38  input: torch.Size([1, 1, 32, 160]) output: torch.Size([41, 1, 37])
39  input: torch.Size([1, 1, 32, 100]) output: torch.Size([26, 1, 37])
```

As shown above, if input is: 32x160 (height x wide), the output will be (41,1,37), where 41 is time steps (remember we use RNN), 37 is the number of classes. If input is 32x100 (h x w), the output will be (26,1,37), where 26 is the time step.

In train.py, CTCLoss is specified as the loss function:

```
1   ...
2   from torch.nn import CTCLoss
3   ...
4   if args.is_use_gpu:
5       crnn = crnn.cuda()
6       criterion = CTCLoss().cuda()
7   else:
8       criterion = CTCLoss()
9   ...
```

The following code snapshot showed the training process (again in train.py):

```
1   for epoch in range(1, args.epoches, 1):
2       #train
3       for p in crnn.parameters():
4           p.requires_grad = True
5       crnn.train()
6       avg_totalLoss=0.0
7       train_acc = 0.0
8       test_acc = 0.0
9       for batch_id, (img_tensor, txt_len, txt_label, txt_name) in tqdm(enumerate( ↩
            trainloader)):
10          #import pdb; pdb.set_trace()
11          optimizer.zero_grad()
12          # img_tensor.shape=torch.Size([4, 1, 32, 100])
13          batch_length = img_tensor.size(0)
14          # https://pytorch.org/docs/stable/nn.html#CTCLoss
```

```
15      # In order to use CuDNN, the following must be satisfied: 'targets' must ←
            be
16      #in a concatenated format.
17      # convert target: txt_label from ( 4, 20 ) -> concatenated form
18      txt_label = txt_label.numpy().reshape(args.max_len*batch_length)
19      # remove 0
20      txt_label = torch.from_numpy(np.array([item for item in txt_label if item ←
            != 0]).astype(np.int))
21      if args.is_use_gpu:
22          img_tensor = Variable(img_tensor.float()).cuda()
23      else:
24          img_tensor = Variable(img_tensor.float())
25      # e.g: txt_len = [4,4,7,6]
26      txt_len = Variable(txt_len.int()).squeeze(1)
27      # e.g: txt_label = [ 5,  6, 17,  2, 33, 18, 22, 31,  9,  4,  8,  5,  2, ←
            8,  9,  6,  5,  3,
28      #   5,  5,  3]
29      txt_label = Variable(txt_label.int())
30
31      # preds shape: torch.Size([26, 4, 37])
32      # 26 means time steps, 4 is batch size, 37 is size of classes
33      preds = crnn(img_tensor)
34      # preds_size : tensor([26, 26, 26, 26]
35      preds_size = Variable(torch.IntTensor([preds.size(0)] * batch_length))
36      total_loss = criterion(preds, txt_label, preds_size, txt_len)
37      total_loss.backward()
38      optimizer.step()
39      # check pred, get max on dim=2 to get prediction
40      _, preds = preds.max(2)
41      preds = preds.transpose(1, 0).contiguous().view(-1)
42      sim_preds = converter.decode(preds.data, preds_size.data, raw=False)
43      for pred, target in zip(sim_preds, txt_name):
44          if pred == target:
45              train_acc += 1
46      avg_totalLoss += total_loss.item()
47      info='epoch : %d ,process: %d/%d ,  totalLoss: %f , lr: %f ' % (epoch, ←
            batch_id, trainloader.__len__(), total_loss.item(), optimizer. ←
            param_groups[0]['lr'])
48      print(info)
49      #break
50  train_acc /= len(dataset)
51  avg_train_acc.append(train_acc)
```

The code above is a quite standard pytorch training procedure.

The only new thing is: **CTCLoss**. It takes 4 inputs:

- log_probs: Tensor of size (T, N, C)(T,N,C),
  where C = number of characters in alphabet including blank, T = input length, and N = batch size.
  The logarithmized probabilities of the outputs (e.g. obtained with torch.nn.functional.log_softmax()).
  In this example, that is the software from our prediction, we got the log_softmax in Line 33, which was calculated in CRNN.py around line 82.

- targets: Tensor of size (N, S)(N,S) or (sum(target_lengths)).
  Targets (cannot be blank). In the second form, the targets are assumed to be concatenated.
  That is the ground truth of target/label data.
  According to pytorch official document:
  https://pytorch.org/docs/stable/nn.html#CTCLoss
  In order to use CuDNN, the following must be satisfied: targets must be in a concatenated format.
  Thus, in line 18 - 29, we concatenate original target from original shape (4,20), where 4 is batch size (as we have 4 training samples, each sample is encoded as a vector of 20 integers), to a shape (21) with current training sample data. And txt_len (in Line 26) stores the length of each sample.

- input_lengths: Tuple or tensor of size (N).
  Lengths of the inputs (must each be $\leq$ T)
  This the length of input (log_probs) must be the size/shape of batches. In this case, will be tensor([26, 26, 26, 26] since we get batch size 4.

- target_lengths: Tuple or tensor of size (N).
  In Line 26, the txt_len stored each batch's target length. In this case, it is: [4,4,7,6] which is summed as 21.
  Now with all those inputs ready, we feed into CTCLoss in Line 36.

The rest of the code is just standard optimizer.backward()/step().

2.2.4 pytorch crnn running results

In this sample, data_sample/ contains 4 sample images. Since the training set is so small, you can run it even on your laptop.

The following showed the steps on how to run it using google's colab.

```
1   ##################################################
2   # how to run this on the google's colab
3   !git clone http://github.com/mingewang/CRNN_OCR.pytorch
4   cd CRNN_OCR.pytorch
5   !git checkout -b comrite origin/comrite
6   !python train.py --epoches 200
7   ##################################################
8
9   find  4  images
10  net has load!
11  0it [00:00, ?it/s]epoch : 1 ,process: 0/1 ,  totalLoss: 15.459192 , lr: 0.001000
12  1it [00:00,  1.37it/s]
13  ------------------------      =>    , gt: 45G1            , False
14  ------------------------      =>    , gt: WHLU            , False
15  ------------------------      =>    , gt: 8374178         , False
16  ------------------------      =>    , gt: 542442          , False
17  epoch : 1 , avg_totalLoss: 15.459192 , lr: 0.001000  avg_test_acc: 0.000000     ↩
        avg_train_acc: 0.000000
18  0it [00:00, ?it/s]epoch : 2 ,process: 0/1 ,  totalLoss: 14.217449 , lr: 0.001000
19  1it [00:00,  1.26it/s]
20  ------------------------      =>    , gt: 45G1            , False
21  ------------------------      =>    , gt: WHLU            , False
22  ------------------------      =>    , gt: 8374178         , False
23  ------------------------      =>    , gt: 542442          , False
24
25
26  epoch : 197 , avg_totalLoss: 0.121996 , lr: 0.000216  avg_test_acc: 0.750000     ↩
        avg_train_acc: 0.750000
27  0it [00:00, ?it/s]epoch : 198 ,process: 0/1 ,  totalLoss: 0.121736 , lr: 0.000216
28  1it [00:00,  1.28it/s]
29  4455-----------------GGG11      => 45G1   , gt: 45G1             , True
30  WWHH-----------------LLUU       => WHLU   , gt: WHLU             , True
31  883377------------4411788       => 8374178 , gt: 8374178         , True
32  544224-----------------2        => 54242  , gt: 542442           , False
33  epoch : 198 , avg_totalLoss: 0.121736 , lr: 0.000216  avg_test_acc: 0.750000     ↩
        avg_train_acc: 0.750000
34  0it [00:00, ?it/s]epoch : 199 ,process: 0/1 ,  totalLoss: 0.120993 , lr: 0.000216
35  1it [00:00,  1.20it/s]
36  4455-----------------GGG11      => 45G1   , gt: 45G1             , True
37  WWHH-----------------LLUU       => WHLU   , gt: WHLU             , True
38  883377------------4411788       => 8374178 , gt: 8374178         , True
```

```
39  544224-------------------2          => 54242   , gt: 542442              , False
40  epoch : 199 , avg_totalLoss: 0.120993 , lr: 0.000216  avg_test_acc: 0.750000      ←
        avg_train_acc: 0.750000
41  0it [00:00, ?it/s]epoch : 200 ,process: 0/1 ,  totalLoss: 0.121136 , lr: 0.000216
42
43  ###############################################
44  # how to download the model from the google's colab
45  from google.colab import files
46  files.download("./model_result/cpu_model_parameter_199.pkl")
47  ###############################################
48
49  !python eval.py --pre_train_model_path ./model_result/cpu_model_parameter_199.pkl
50  net has load!
51  4455-------------------GG11         => 45G1
52  WWHH-------------------LLUU         => WHLU
53  883377--------------4411778         => 8374178
54  54422444----------------22          => 54242
```

You may be noticed that the last one is not correct, a 4 is missing. With a large training data set, we should be able to overcome that issue.

2.3   More OCR references and models

Powered by CRNN/CTCLoss and large data set, we can build a reasonable good OCR system as shown in:

https://github.com/Sierkinhane/crnn_chinese_characters_rec

Some other people used a pre-trained image model + CTCLoss to do the OCR, for example:

https://github.com/zhiqwang/crnn.pytorch

Here are some more references/documents about OCR/CTC:

https://www.cs.toronto.edu/~graves/icml_2006.pdf

https://towardsdatascience.com/intuitively-understanding-connectionist-temporal-classification-3797e43a86c

2.4   summary

In this chapter, we learned how to build a modern end-to-end OCR system using deep learning technologies. In particular, you should:

- have a basic understanding of an OCR system.

- know how to use opencv extract line and word.

- understand how CTC works, and how to use pytorch CTCLoss function.

- be able to understand and use several OCR systems on github.

- be able to build/train your own OCR system with CTC (advanced level).

Chapter 3

Audio processing, speech processing

Audio processing is a broad term. Anything related to audio can be categorized there. Here, we mainly refer to speech processing, more specifically we refer to speech recognition/voice recognition, speaker recognition etc.

Let's first clarify many confusing terms.

- **speech recognition** refers to technologies that enables the recognition and translation of spoken language into text by computers. It is also known as **automatic speech recognition (ASR)**, **computer speech recognition** or **speech to text (STT)**.

- **speaker recognition** is used to answer the question "who is speaking?". It normally has two phases: enrollment and verification. While during the enrollment phrase, the speaker's voice is recorded, during verification case, a speech sample is compared against previously recorded voice.
Speaker recognition system can fall into two categories: text-dependent and text-independent. If the text must be the same for enrollment and verification, this is called **text-dependent** recognition. Otherwise, **text-independent** recognition.

There are normally two major applications for speaker recognition: **speaker verification/speaker authentication**, and **speaker identification**.
Identification is different from verification. For example, If the speaker claims to be of a certain identity and the voice is used to verify this claim, this is called verification or authentication. On the other hand, identification is the task of determining an unknown speaker's identity. Text-independent system are normally used for identification, while the text-dependent system is used for verification/authentication applications.

- **speaker diarisation** is the process of partitioning an input audio stream into homogeneous segments according to the speaker's identity.

- **voice recognition** can refer to speaker recognition or speech recognition depending on the context. We tend to use voice recognition as speech recognition.

Just as we see a big rise of AI/deep learning technologies in the fields of image/video, NLP in recent years, we see similar trends appear in the audio world.

In this chapter, we will show you how deep learning is applied to speech-related areas.

3.1   how to handle audio signals in DNN?

Traditionally, we use hand-crafted features e.g.: **spectrogram/MFCC** to pre-process audio signals.

Recently, some people tried to use raw waveforms directly.

Let's walk through those two approaches.

3.1.1   feeding raw audio directly, end-to-end approach

For audio/speech related machine learning tasks, we can feed those time-domain data (raw audio samples) directly into DNN, let network learn those low-level speech representations directly from waveforms.

One advantage is: it potentially allows the network to better capture important narrow-band speaker characteristics, such as pitch, formants, etc.

Some researchers are exploring those possibilities. For example, Mirco Ravanelli etc supposed a promising neural network called **SincNet** to do the speaker identification/verification directly on raw audio using pytorch. See more details at: http://github.com/mravanelli/SincNet

Neil etc proposed "End-to-End Speech Recognition From the Raw Waveform".
(see https://arxiv.org/abs/1806.07098).

3.1.2   spectrogram/MFCC, hand-crafted features for audio

When we speak, we generate sound signals changing over time.

This changing over time is called **frequency**. **Hertz (Hz)** is defined as one cycle per second to measure frequency. The human hearing range is around 20Hz to 20kHz.

A **spectrogram** shows the spectrum of frequencies (varying with time) of a signal visually. When applied to an audio signal, spectrograms are sometimes called **sonographs, voiceprints, or voicegrams**.

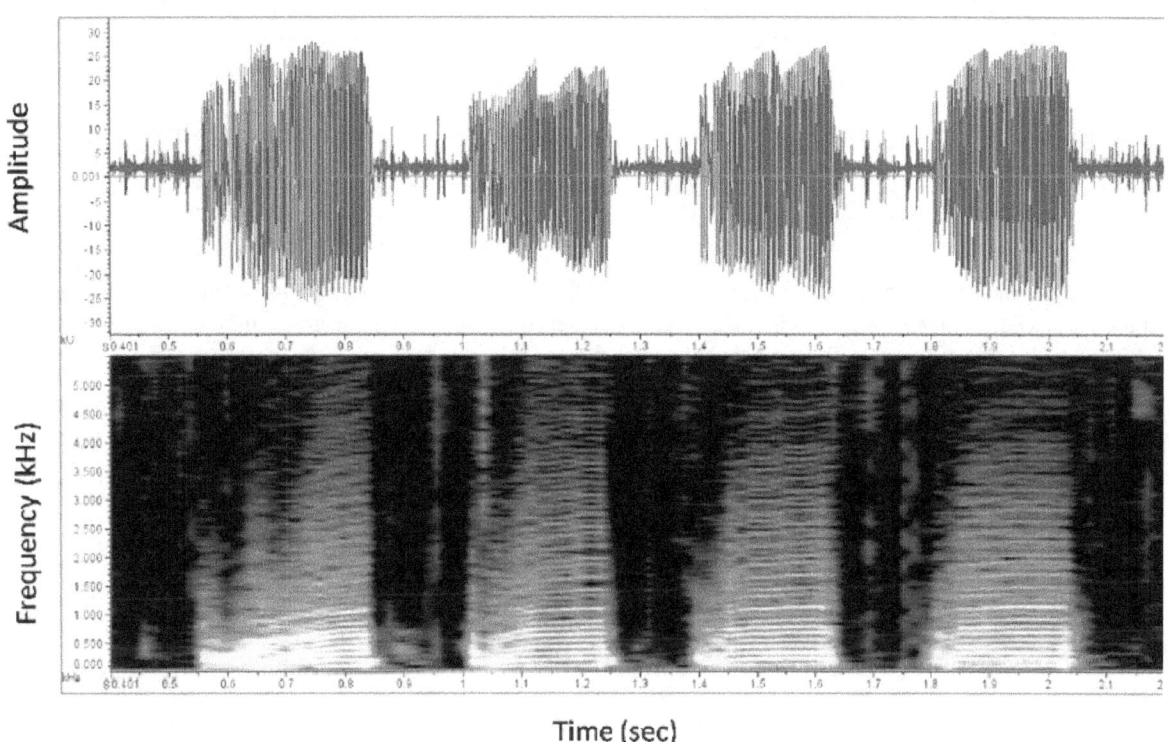

Figure 3.1: oscillogram and spectrogram

The upper blue-colored plot in the above figure is an oscillogram, presenting the waveform and amplitude of the sound over time, The X-axis is Time (sec) and the Y-axis is Amplitude.

The lower plot in the figure is a plot of the sounds' frequency over time, The X-axis is Time (sec) and the Y-axis is Frequency (kHz). The amount of energy present in each frequency is represented by the intensity of the color. The brighter the color, the more energy is present in the sound at that frequency.

Tip

What is the difference between spectrum and spectrogram?

A spectrum shows the frequency content of an entire signal, while a spectrogram shows how the frequency content of a signal changes over time.

Let's say, we have signal last from (0, T), we can think of a spectrum as taking Fourier Transform over the whole period of time (0,T); while for spectrogram, we split the signal into many time-slice chunks (0,t1,t2,...,tn), then we apply local Fourier Transform on each chunk, thus a spectrogram can be thought of a visual representation of those Short-Time Fourier Transforms.

The sound/audio signals stored/used in computers is normally a recording of the oscillogram of our voice.

People found it is beneficial to convert oscillogram to spectrograms for speech processing, especially for speech recognition. The intuition is: a spectrogram is a representation of the audio signal in the time-frequency domain, it contains both time and frequency information, thus it is probably good to be used as a feature-set for such signals.

Normally, we group the incoming audio samples into short segments, for example, 20 milliseconds long. Then we calculate the strength of the frequencies for each segment, essentially, we get the spectrogram of this audio stream. Lastly, we use this spectrogram as the feature set to feed into DNN.

As human ear is more sensitive to some frequencies than others, spectrogram can be further processed/optimized as another representation called **Mel-Frequency Cepstral Coefficients (MFCCs)**, which is based on a linear cosine transform of a log power spectrum on a nonlinear Mel scale of frequency.

We call spectrogram/MFCC the hand-crafted features.

In short, the spectrogram is a quite useful tool to handle speech/audio related machine learning tasks.

3.1.3   how to feed hand-crafted features into a DNN

One way of doing this is: we can treat those spectrogram/MFCC as sequence data, then feed them into RNN. Many speech applications, such as speech to text, treat these audio signals this way.

Also, we can treat the spectrogram/MFCC as image data. If you observe the previous spectrogram figure carefully, both spectrogram and MFCC can be treated as a two-dimensional grey-scale image. (Time and frequency can be think as a point in2-D plane (x,y), the strength of the frequency can be treated as grey-scale info), Thus, we can feed that data into a CNN network.

With that background, we can do some real speech-related projects.

3.2   audio classification example

Imagine, if a machine can understand our simple words, it will open up lots of applications.

Google/TensorFlow published a tutorial to classify a one-second audio clip as either silence, an unknown word, yes, no, up, down, left, right, on, off, stop, or go, etc.

It also released a free speech commands datasets, which includes 65,000 one-second long utterances of 30 short words by thousands of different people. This data set is quite useful to build an audio/voice classifier.

Google's tutorial uses tensorflow and it achieved an accuracy between 85% and 90%.

More details at:
https://www.tensorflow.org/tutorials/sequences/audio_recognition

In this chapter, we try to use pytorch to do the same thing. The original git repo is at:
https://github.com/tugstugi/pytorch-speech-commands

I updated to pytorch 1.0, and put it into a comrite branch:

https://github.com/mingewang/pytorch-speech-commands

You can read the code at:

https://github.com/mingewang/pytorch-speech-commands/tree/comrite

The main idea of this example is:
we convert raw audio file/stream into a spectrogram, treat them as image data, then feed them into CNN to do the classification.

3.2.1   pytorch-speech-commands source code analysis

Most of the code is quite straightforward to understand.

The datasets/speech_commands_dataset.py defines a standard pytorch dataset using google's speech commands data.

Several models are defined under models/.

```
1  (pytorch_env) pytorch-speech-commands$ ls models/
2  densenet.py  dpn.py  __init__.py  __pycache__  resnet.py  resnext.py  vgg.py  ←
       wideresnet.py
```

The main training process code is in: train_speech_commands.py.

I put some code snap as following to highlight how is trained:

```
1    ...
2    ...
3
4    data_aug_transform = Compose([ChangeAmplitude(), ChangeSpeedAndPitchAudio(),  ↵
         FixAudioLength(), ToSTFT(), StretchAudioOnSTFT(), TimeshiftAudioOnSTFT(),  ↵
         FixSTFTDimension()])
5    bg_dataset = BackgroundNoiseDataset(args.background_noise, data_aug_transform)
6    add_bg_noise = AddBackgroundNoiseOnSTFT(bg_dataset)
7    train_feature_transform = Compose([ToMelSpectrogramFromSTFT(n_mels=n_mels),  ↵
         DeleteSTFT(), ToTensor('mel_spectrogram', 'input')])
8    train_dataset = SpeechCommandsDataset(args.train_dataset,
9                                  Compose([LoadAudio(),
10                                            data_aug_transform,
11                                            add_bg_noise,
12                                            train_feature_transform]))
13
14   ...
15
16   weights = train_dataset.make_weights_for_balanced_classes()
17   sampler = WeightedRandomSampler(weights, len(weights))
18   train_dataloader = DataLoader(train_dataset, batch_size=args.batch_size, sampler= ↵
         sampler,
19                                  pin_memory=use_gpu, num_workers=args. ↵
                                       dataload_workers_nums)
20
21   ...
22   ...
23
24   def train(epoch):
25       global global_step
26
27       print("epoch %3d with lr=%.02e" % (epoch, get_lr()))
28       phase = 'train'
29       writer.add_scalar('%s/learning_rate' % phase,  get_lr(), epoch)
30
31       model.train()  # Set model to training mode
32
33       running_loss = 0.0
```

```
34      it = 0
35      correct = 0
36      total = 0
37
38      pbar = tqdm(train_dataloader, unit="audios", unit_scale=train_dataloader. ↵
            batch_size)
39      for batch in pbar:
40          inputs = batch['input']
41          inputs = torch.unsqueeze(inputs, 1)
42          targets = batch['target']
43
44          if args.mixup:
45              inputs, targets = mixup(inputs, targets, num_classes=len(CLASSES))
46
47          inputs = Variable(inputs, requires_grad=True)
48          targets = Variable(targets, requires_grad=False)
49
50          if use_gpu:
51              inputs = inputs.cuda()
52              targets = targets.cuda()
53
54          # forward/backward
55          outputs = model(inputs)
56          if args.mixup:
57              loss = mixup_cross_entropy_loss(outputs, targets)
58          else:
59              loss = criterion(outputs, targets)
60          optimizer.zero_grad()
61          loss.backward()
62          optimizer.step()
63
64          # statistics
65          it += 1
66          global_step += 1
67          running_loss += loss.data.item()
68          pred = outputs.data.max(1, keepdim=True)[1]
69          if args.mixup:
70              targets = batch['target']
71              targets = Variable(targets, requires_grad=False).cuda()
72          correct += pred.eq(targets.data.view_as(pred)).sum()
73          total += targets.size(0)
74
```

```
75          writer.add_scalar('%s/loss' % phase, loss.data.item(), global_step)
76
77          # update the progress bar
78          pbar.set_postfix({
79              'loss': "%.05f" % (running_loss / it),
80              'acc': "%.02f%%" % (100*correct/total)
81          })
82
83      accuracy = correct/total
84      epoch_loss = running_loss / it
85      writer.add_scalar('%s/accuracy' % phase, 100*accuracy, epoch)
86      writer.add_scalar('%s/epoch_loss' % phase, epoch_loss, epoch)
```

- Line 4-12, we load the data set.
  Notice we do some data arguments and preprocessing first, and finally, convert to MFCC. Those utilities are defined in transforms/transforms_stft.py and transforms/transforms_wav.py.

- Line 16-19, we load the dataset into pytorch standard dataloader.

- Line 24-86 defined a standard pytorch training process code.

3.2.2 run/result

Depending on your machines, it could take several hours to train.

You easily run it at google's colab (GPU enabled env), as shown in the following code:

```
1   #############################################################################
2   # running on google's colab
3   !pip install tensorboardX
4   !git clone https://github.com/mingewang/pytorch-speech-commands
5   cd pytorch-speech-commands
6   !git checkout -b comrite origin/comrite
7
8   !./download_speech_commands_dataset.sh
9
10  !python train_speech_commands.py --model=vgg19_bn --optim=sgd  \
11    --lr-scheduler=plateau --learning-rate=0.01 --lr-scheduler-patience=5 \
12    --max-epochs=70 --batch-size=96
```

```
13   ###################################################################
14
15   use_gpu True
16   training vgg19_bn for Google speech commands...
17   epoch    0 with lr=1.00e-02
18   100% 56256/56256 [06:35<00:00, 193.65audios/s, loss=1.52037, acc=46.00%]
19     0% 0/7488 [00:00<?, ?audios/s]train_speech_commands.py:208:
20   UserWarning: volatile was removed and now has no effect. Use `with torch.no_grad ↩
        ():` instead.
21     inputs = Variable(inputs, volatile = True)
22   100% 7488/7488 [00:19<00:00, 379.35audios/s, loss=0.92267, acc=72.00%]
23   total time elapsed: 0h 6m 59s , best accuracy: 0.00%, best loss 0.922667
24   epoch    1 with lr=1.00e-02
25   100% 56256/56256 [06:22<00:00, 146.98audios/s, loss=0.64335, acc=80.00%]
26   100% 7488/7488 [00:18<00:00, 534.87audios/s, loss=0.64509, acc=78.00%]
27   total time elapsed: 0h 13m 45s , best accuracy: 0.00%, best loss 0.645094
28   epoch    2 with lr=1.00e-02
29
30   ...
31   ...
32
33   epoch   67 with lr=1.00e-08
34   100% 56256/56256 [07:19<00:00, 361.31audios/s, loss=0.20666, acc=94.00%]
35   100% 7488/7488 [00:21<00:00, 345.68audios/s, loss=0.10415, acc=97.00%]
36   total time elapsed: 8h 4m 13s , best accuracy: 0.00%, best loss 0.100655
37   epoch   68 with lr-1.00c-08
38   100% 56256/56256 [07:13<00:00, 129.76audios/s, loss=0.21583, acc=94.00%]
39   100% 7488/7488 [00:21<00:00, 346.66audios/s, loss=0.10791, acc=97.00%]
40   total time elapsed: 8h 11m 49s , best accuracy: 0.00%, best loss 0.100655
41   epoch   69 with lr=1.00e-08
42   100% 56256/56256 [07:36<00:00, 184.92audios/s, loss=0.20579, acc=94.00%]
43   100% 7488/7488 [00:22<00:00, 490.04audios/s, loss=0.10658, acc=97.00%]
44   total time elapsed: 8h 19m 49s , best accuracy: 0.00%, best loss 0.100655
45   finished
```

The accurate rate is around 97%, it is quite good.

As Andrew Ng point it out a long time ago: if speech recognition can go from 95% accurate to 99% accurate, it will become a primary way to interact with computers. **This 4% accuracy gap is the difference between annoyingly unreliable and incredibly useful**.

Interesting readers can read more references at:

3.3   automatic speech recognition (voice recognition)

Speech recognition is a quite useful building block for many interesting applications:

- Telecommunications: Command-and-Control, agents, call center automation, customer care, voice calling.

- Office/desktop: voice navigation of desktop, voice browser for the Internet, voice dialer, dictation.

- Manufacturing business: package sorting, data entry, form filling.

- Medical/legal: the creation of stylized reports.

- Game/aids-to-the-handicapped: voice control of selective features of the game, the wheelchair, the environment (climate control).

- speech transcriptions

- Word spotting/trigger word

- Speaker identification/verification

- Amazon Alexa, Google Home, etc.

It usually has the following architecture/pipeline:

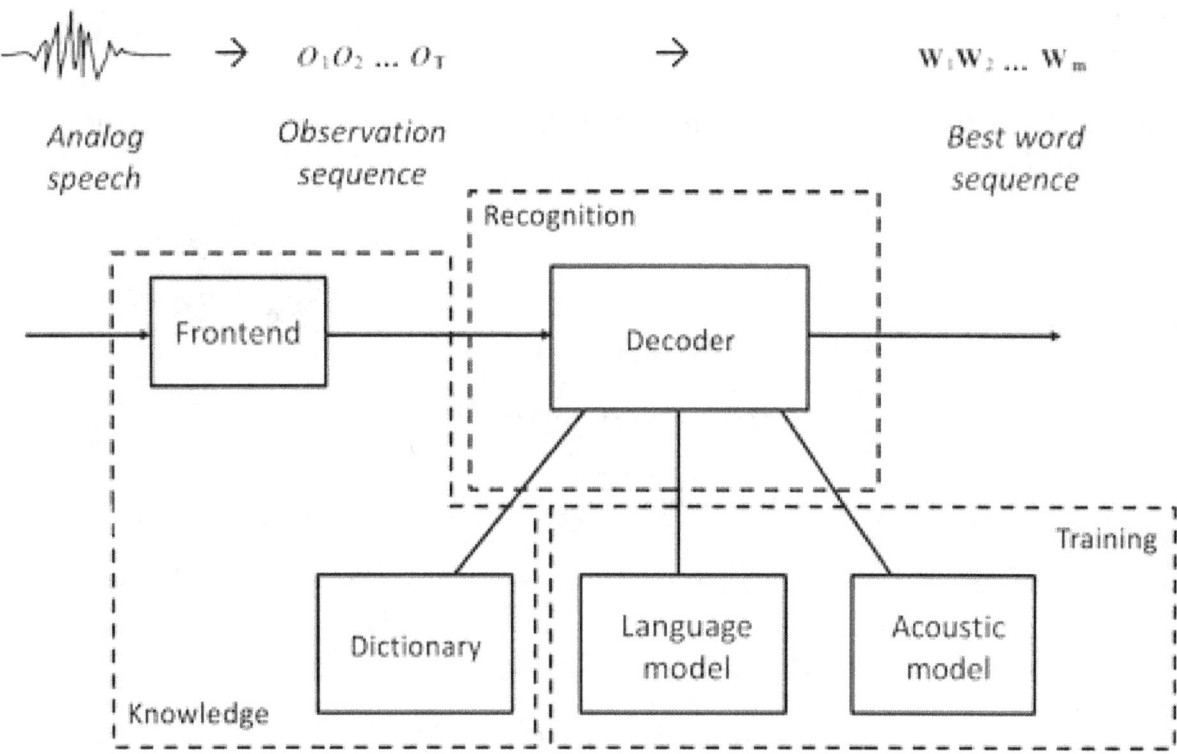

Figure 3.2: speech recognition pipeline

Before 2000s, it was dominated by traditional approaches such as Hidden Markov Models (HMM).

As shown in the figure above, an **acoustic model** represents the relationship between an audio signal and the phonemes or other linguistic units that make up speech.

A **language model** is a probability distribution over sequences of words, provides context to distinguish between words and phrases that sound similar.

Approximately, a front-end will convert the raw speech signals into features such as MFCC representations, those features will then be fed into a acoustic model to get phonemes, the decoder will use that phonemes information, with the help from a language model to find the The most likely sequence of words, thus decodes the speech signal into text.

Nowadays, many parts of the pipeline have been taken over by RNN/LSTM, which avoids the vanishing gradient problem and can learn **long-distance dependence** tasks which require memories of events that happened thousands of discrete time steps ago.

Remember, we can treat spectrogram/MFCC as sequence data, then feed them into RNN layers, so a naive speech recognition engine could look like the following:

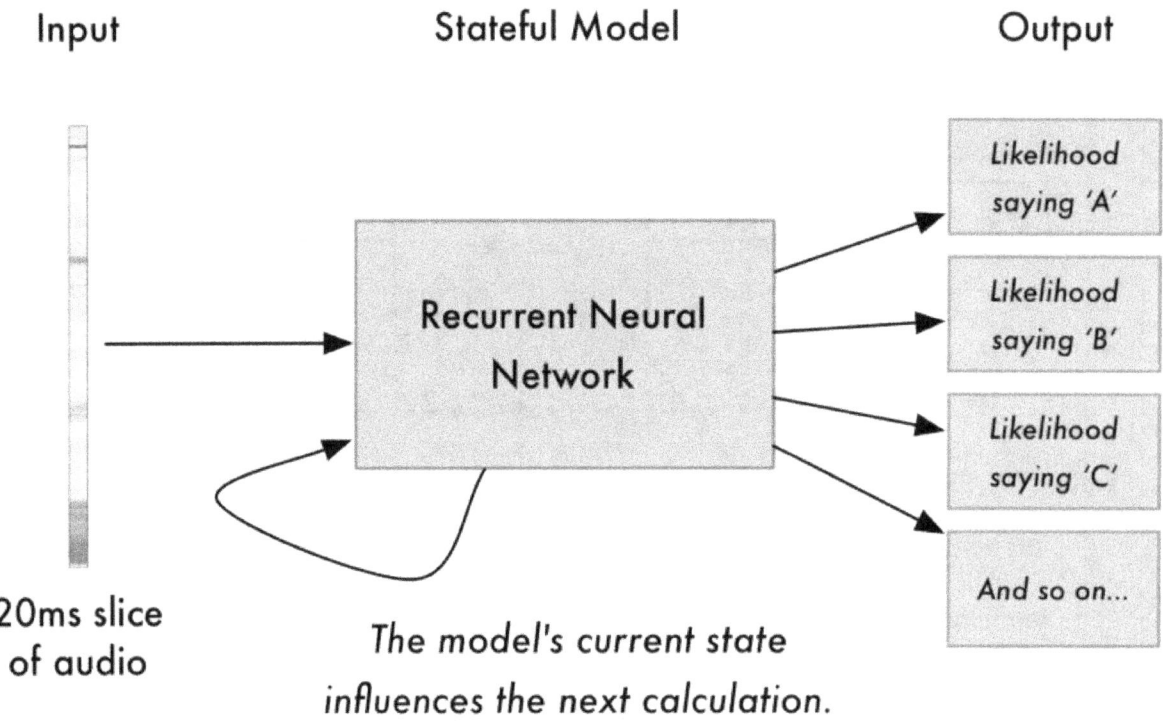

Figure 3.3: spectrogram to RNN

The output may look like the following:

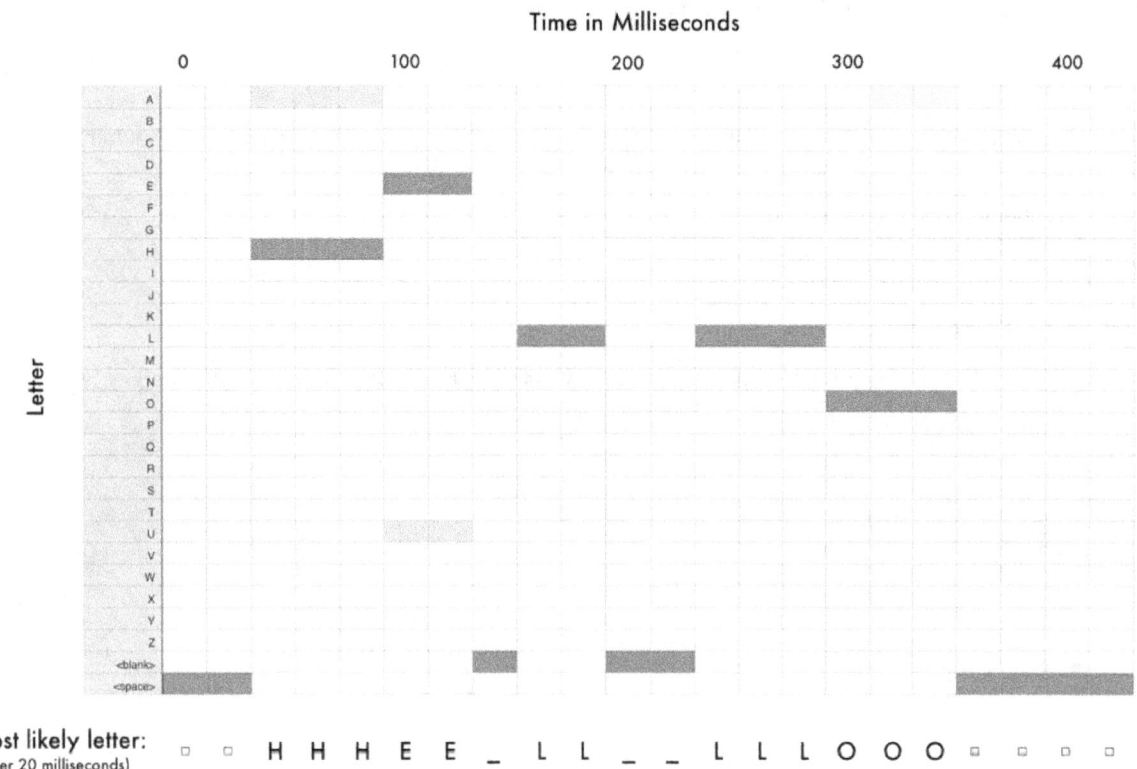

Figure 3.4: spectrogram to RNN output

Combining with CTC we learned from OCR, it is possible for us to build a reasonable speech recognition system using the above architecture.

Actually, baidu/mozilla's deep speech is quite similar to that from a very high-level point of view.

3.3.1 Deepspeech - Mozilla's open source ASR

A little bit history here:

Around 2007, LSTM trained by Connectionist Temporal Classification (CTC) started to outperform traditional speech recognition in certain applications.

Since 2014, there has been much research interest in "end-to-end" ASR which aims to get rid of those components in the pipeline.

Around 2014-2015, baidu/google reported a dramatic performance improvement using CTC-trained LSTM. Baidu published their deepspeech (v1/v2/v3) since then.

In 2017, Mozilla released open-sourced DeepSpeech project which is based on work from Baidu's Deepspeech and tensorflow.

It claims that the transcription engine has an error rate of just 6.5 percent, which is very close to what humans can do. It means new apps should be better at recognizing what users have to say than earlier products.

More details about deepspeech can be found at:
https://research.mozilla.org/machine-learning/
https://github.com/mozilla/DeepSpeech

Get excited? Let's see how we can use it.

We can use it to train a new set of data, or use the pre-trained data to do the speech-to-text right away.

Using pre-trained ASR is quite easy, as shown in the following:

```
1  (tensorflow)$ pip3 install deepspeech
2  (tensorflow)$ wget -O - https://github.com/mozilla/DeepSpeech/releases/download/ ↵
       v0.3.0/deepspeech-0.3.0-models.tar.gz | tar xvfz -
3
4  # you should see similar like this
5  (tensorflow):$ ls -l models/
6  total 2.7G
7  -rw-r--r-- 1 mwang mwang  329 Sep 18 09:10 alphabet.txt
8  -rw-r--r-- 1 mwang mwang 1.7G Sep 18 09:10 lm.binary
9  -rw-r--r-- 1 mwang mwang 181M Sep 18 08:52 output_graph.pb
10 -rw-r--r-- 1 mwang mwang 181M Sep 18 08:52 output_graph.pbmm
11 -rw-r--r-- 1 mwang mwang 181M Sep 18 08:52 output_graph.rounded.pb
12 -rw-r--r-- 1 mwang mwang 181M Sep 18 08:52 output_graph.rounded.pbmm
13 -rw-r--r-- 1 mwang mwang 264M Oct  9 03:55 trie
14
15 # now we can try an audio file
16 (tensorflow):$
17 deepspeech --model models/output_graph.pbmm --alphabet models/alphabet.txt \
18     --lm models/lm.binary --trie models/trie --audio my_audio_file.wav
```

It should output a transcribed text.

3.3.2 facebook's wav2letter

Another alternative approach are **attention-based** models.

They were introduced simultaneously by Chan et al. of Carnegie Mellon University, Google Brain and Bahdanaua et al. of the University of Montreal in 2016.

In 2018, Facebook release its attention-based speech recognition project wav2letter at:
https://github.com/facebookresearch/wav2letter/

At this moment, it is quite involving to even get the pre-trained model working, but it is doable if you follow online instructions carefully.

Tip
The accurate rate of wav2letter is similar to deepspeech at the time of writing, but deepspeech is much easier/-faster to use.

3.3.3 kaldi

Kaldi is a toolkit for speech recognition written in C++ and licensed under the Apache License v2.0. The learning curve of kaldi is quite steep, but it is quite flexible, which is intended and suited for use by **speech recognition researchers**.

Based on my personal experience, the pre-trained kaldi (https://github.com/gooofy/zamia-speech) seems provide better accuracy and faster speed than deepspeech/wav2letter, so it is worth to try.

To get started, you may read:

https://kaldi-asr.org/doc/kaldi_for_dummies.html

https://kaldi-asr.org/doc/tutorial.html

Kaldi code is at:

https://github.com/kaldi-asr/kaldi

They also provide some pre-trained models for ASR, speaker identification, speaker verification, language model at:

https://kaldi-asr.org/models.html

More documents about kaldi could be found at:

http://kaldi-asr.org/doc/

3.4　pytorch torchaudio domain library

Just at the time of writing, pytorch released 1.2 with **torchaudio** 0.3 on Aug, 8, 2019.

It supports reading/loading a .wav file, and have some built-in transformations to calculate Spectrogram , MFCC etc. Also it added support for Kaldi!

It is so new, I have not spent time exploring it yet. Interesting readers can get started at:

https://pytorch.org/tutorials/beginner/audio_preprocessing_tutorial.html

3.5　summary

Speech/speaker recognition etc is still not a solved field, actually a quite challenging area. For example, many speech system's performances/accuracy drops dramatically in a noisy environment, this is still a very active research area.

Anyway, after reading this chapter, you should know:

- the concepts of speech recognition, speaker recognition, speaker diarisation etc.

- what are spectrogram/MFCC etc hand-crafted features for speech signals.

- how to feed hand-crafted features into a DNN.

- how to use pre-trained ASR models.

Advanced readers may be able to build their own ASR systems!

Chapter 4

Autoencoder network

All DNNs we learned so far from previous chapters need labeled training data set, that is why they are called **supervised learning**.

What if we do not have labeled training data? How can machines learn in those cases?

Un-supervised learning will try to address those challenges.

In this chapter, we will introduce **autoencoder network**, which does not need any labeled training data!

Wikipedia has such a precise description on this, so I quote it here:

https://en.wikipedia.org/wiki/Autoencoder

```
1  An autoencoder is a type of artificial neural network used to
2  learn efficient data codings in an unsupervised manner.
3
4  The aim of an autoencoder is to learn a representation (encoding)
5  for a set of data, typically for dimensionality reduction,
6  by training the network to ignore signal "noise."
7
8  Along with the reduction side, a reconstructing side is learned,
9  where the autoencoder tries to generate from the reduced encoding
10 a representation as close as possible to its original input, hence its name.
11
```

```
12   Recently, the autoencoder concept has become more widely used
13   for learning generative models of data. Some of the most powerful AI
14   in the 2010s have involved sparse autoencoders stacked
15   inside of deep neural networks.
```

The key concept of the autoencoder is: **the target data are the same as or generated from the input data, so we do not need to collect target labels.**

Sometimes, people categorize autoencoder as a **self-supervised** technique.

In this chapter, we will first show how autoencoder works, then we will demo some cool applications of autoencoder: data denoising, auto-generate data etc.

4.1   how autoencoder works?

Let's look at the architecture of the autoencoder network:

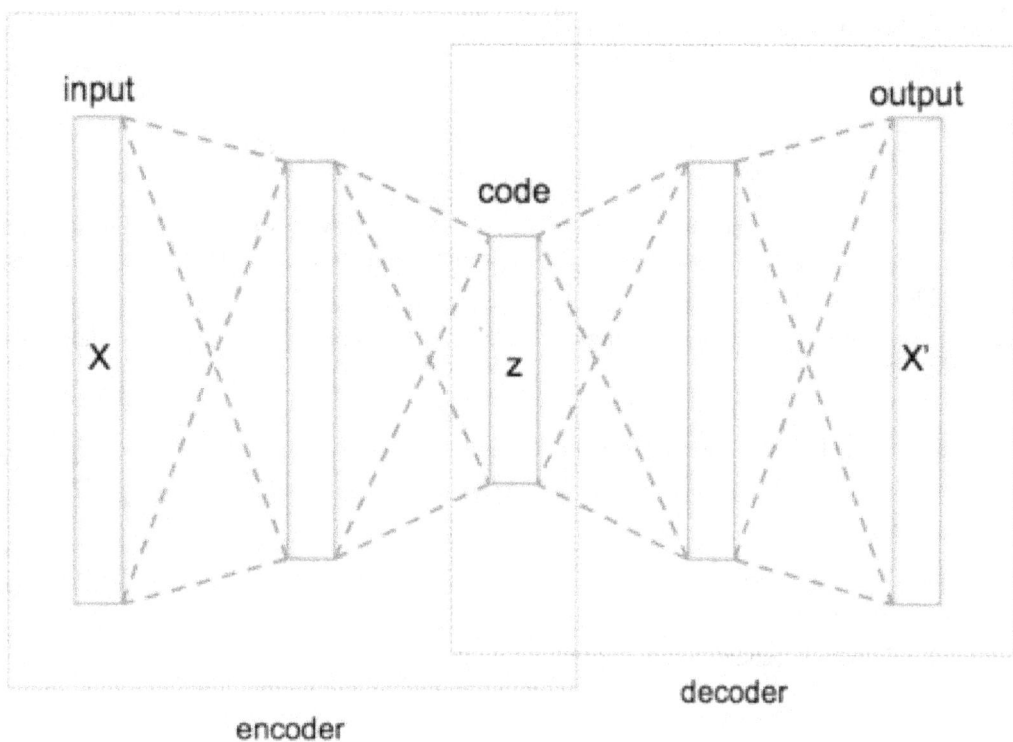

Figure 4.1: autoencoder architecture

As shown in the figure, an autoencoder network has two connected networks, one is an encoder which takes in an input, and converts it into a smaller, dense representation; the other is a decoder network, which converts the dense representation back to the original input.

Since the code/encoding (z as shown in the figure) has far fewer units than the input, the encoder must learn to preserve as much of the relevant information as possible in the limited encoding and intelligently discard irrelevant parts. While the decoder must learn to take the encoding and properly reconstruct it.

Normally, we train an encoder and decoder together. The **reconstruction loss** function could be either the mean-squared error or cross-entropy between the output and the input etc.

With proper training, the autoencoder can learn the essential part of the representation of our dataset, and can be applied to very interesting applications.

4.2 Data Denoising

As we know, autoencoders can learn data's representation.

One interesting application is: we can use it to remove the noise from the data set. How?

The main idea is:
we add some noises to our original input, feed them into the autoencoder network with our original clean input as the target. Once it is trained, this network should have the capability to remove noises. The official term for this is called **data denoising**.

Let's see an example of how to do the data denoising using MNIST data. A relative simple/easy to understand can be found at:
https://github.com/Abhipanda4/Denoising-Autoencoders

I updated to pytorch 1.0, and put into a comrite branch:
https://github.com/mingewang/Denoising-Autoencoders

You can read the code at:
https://github.com/mingewang/Denoising-Autoencoders/tree/comrite

The code is easy to understand.

Here is the code of encoder and decoder:

```
1   import torch
2   import torch.nn as nn
3   import torch.nn.functional as F
4
5
6   class DenoisingAutoencoder(nn.Module):
7       def __init__(self, n_inp):
8           super(DenoisingAutoencoder, self).__init__()
9           n_hidden = 600
10          self.encoder = nn.Linear(n_inp, n_hidden)
```

```
11          self.decoder = nn.Linear(n_hidden, n_inp)
12
13      def forward(self, x):
14          encoded = F.relu(self.encoder(x))
15          decoded = torch.sigmoid(self.decoder(encoded))
16          return decoded
```

The following is the main training code:

```
1   import torch
2   import torch.nn as nn
3   import torch.nn.functional as F
4   import torch.optim as optim
5   from torch.autograd import Variable
6   from torchvision import datasets, transforms
7
8   import os
9   import matplotlib.pyplot as plt
10  import numpy as np
11
12  from model import DenoisingAutoencoder
13
14  device = torch.device('cuda' if torch.cuda.is_available() else 'cpu')
15  print("using device:", device)
16
17  # global constants
18  BATCH_SIZE = 32
19  N_INP = 784
20  N_EPOCHS = 10
21  NOISE = 0.5
22
23  # MNIST data loading
24  root = './data'
25  if not os.path.exists(root):
26      os.mkdir(root)
27
28  trans = transforms.Compose([transforms.ToTensor()])
29  train_set = datasets.MNIST(root=root, train=True, transform=trans, download=True)
30  test_set = datasets.MNIST(root=root, train=False, transform=trans, download=True)
31
32  train_loader = torch.utils.data.DataLoader(
```

```
33          dataset=train_set,
34          batch_size=BATCH_SIZE,
35          shuffle=True)
36
37  test_loader = torch.utils.data.DataLoader(
38          dataset=test_set,
39          batch_size=BATCH_SIZE,
40          shuffle=False)
41
42  # support GPU
43  # need to model to device, and batch data to device
44  auto_encoder = DenoisingAutoencoder(N_INP).to(device)
45  optimizer = optim.Adam(auto_encoder.parameters(), lr=1e-3)
46  criterion = nn.MSELoss()
47
48  # set plot and view data for visualization
49  N_COLS = 8
50  N_ROWS = 4
51  view_data = []
52  for i in range(N_ROWS * N_COLS):
53      noise = np.random.choice([1, 0], size=(28, 28), p=[NOISE, 1 - NOISE])
54      view_data.append( ( test_set[i][0] * torch.FloatTensor(noise)).to(device) )
55  plt.figure(figsize=(20, 4))
56
57  for epoch in range(N_EPOCHS):
58      for b_index, (x, _) in enumerate(train_loader):
59          # need to add batch data to device
60          y = x.view(x.size()[0], -1).to(device)
61          noise = np.random.choice([1, 0], size=(BATCH_SIZE, N_INP), p=[NOISE, 1 -  ↩
              NOISE])
62          inp = y * ( torch.FloatTensor(noise).to(device) )
63          decoded = auto_encoder(inp)
64          loss = criterion(decoded,y)
65          optimizer.zero_grad()
66          loss.backward()
67          optimizer.step()
68
69      print("Epoch: [%3d], Loss: %.4f" %(epoch + 1, loss.data))
70
71  for i in range(N_ROWS * N_COLS):
72      # original image
73      r = i // N_COLS
```

```
74        c = i % N_COLS + 1
75        ax = plt.subplot(2 * N_ROWS, N_COLS, 2 * r * N_COLS + c)
76        plt.imshow( view_data[i].squeeze().cpu() )
77        plt.gray()
78        ax.get_xaxis().set_visible(False)
79        ax.get_yaxis().set_visible(False)
80
81        # reconstructed image
82        ax = plt.subplot(2 * N_ROWS, N_COLS, 2 * r * N_COLS + c + N_COLS)
83        x = Variable(view_data[i])
84        y = auto_encoder(x.view(1, -1)).cpu()
85        plt.imshow( y.detach().squeeze().numpy().reshape(28, 28))
86        plt.gray()
87        ax.get_xaxis().set_visible(False)
88        ax.get_yaxis().set_visible(False)
89 plt.show()
```

- Line 57 - 67 showed the training process.

- Line 61 - 62 we added some noises to the input

- Line 73 - 64, we feed the noised input into out model/auto-encoder, then calculate the loss between the input and target which is noised input.

- Line 71 - 88, we visualize some testing data.

The running result was:

```
1  (pytorch_env) $ python ./train.py
2  using device: cpu
3  Epoch: [  1], Loss: 0.0159
4  Epoch: [  2], Loss: 0.0144
5  Epoch: [  3], Loss: 0.0102
6  Epoch: [  4], Loss: 0.0110
7  Epoch: [  5], Loss: 0.0105
8  Epoch: [  6], Loss: 0.0104
9  Epoch: [  7], Loss: 0.0101
10 Epoch: [  8], Loss: 0.0104
11 Epoch: [  9], Loss: 0.0100
12 Epoch: [ 10], Loss: 0.0103
```

And the graph showed:

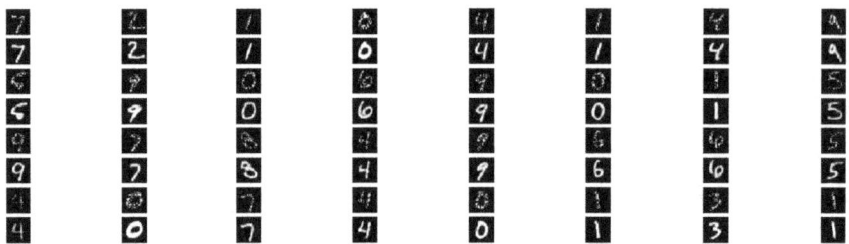

Figure 4.2: data denoising

In the figure above, the odd line in the graph is the noisy input, the even line is our reconstructed output.

We just used a very simple two-layer (encoder/decoder) model, but the result looks pretty good. This clearly showed the power of an autoencoder!

4.3 Data Auto generation

Another cool application is to use a variant of autoencoder called **variational autoencoder (VAE)** to generate data.

VAE is a powerful generative model, it has many interesting applications such as: generating fake human faces (see a graph below), producing purely synthetic music, etc.

The following graph showed some faces generated by VAE. It is hard to tell if a face is faked or real.

Figure 4.3: fake faces generated using VAE

So what is a variational autoencoder?

The basic idea of a VAE is: we use an autoencoder to learn a **latent variable** model from the input data, then we pick a data point z in that latent space, use the decoder to re-generate data from z.

The following figure shows a VAE architecture:

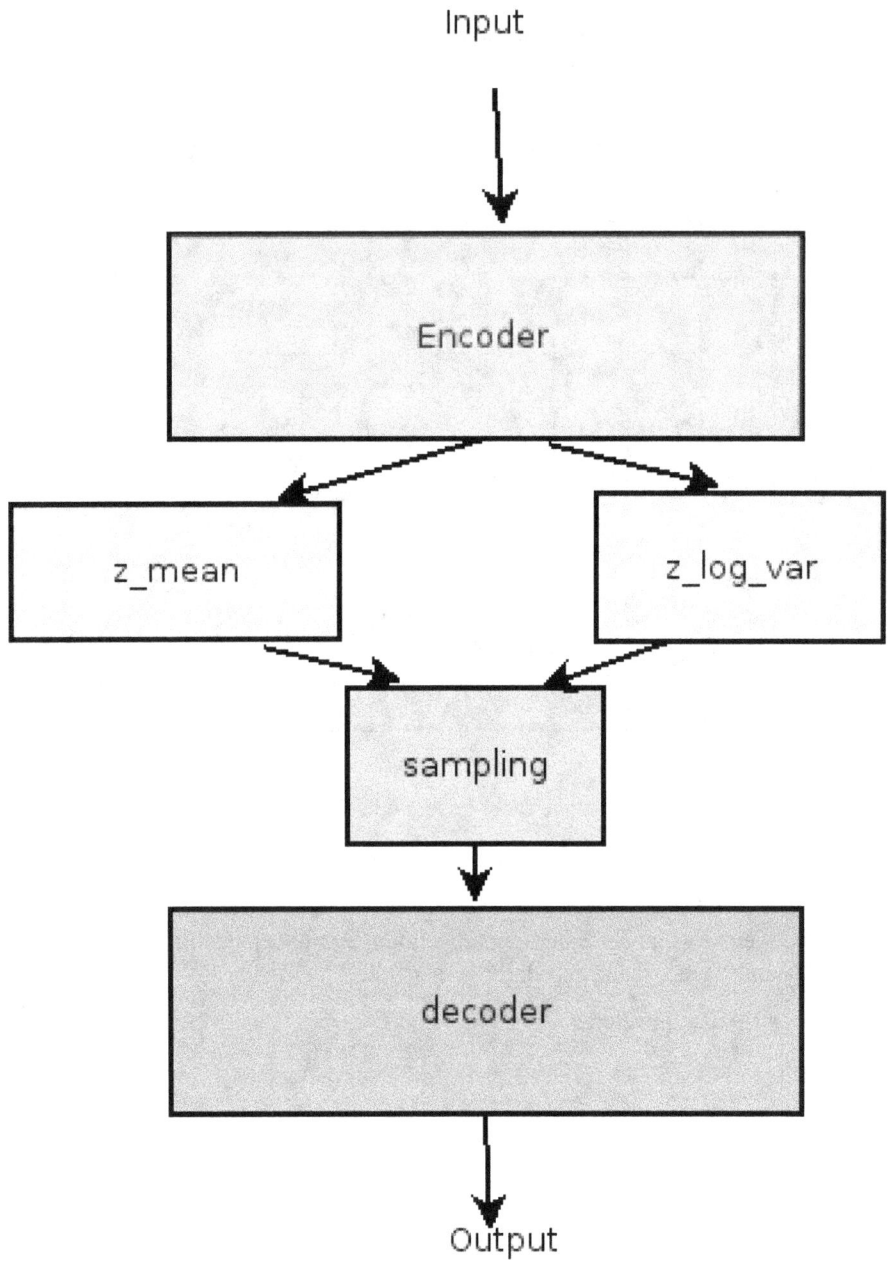

Figure 4.4: variational autoencoder architecture

As shown in the figure, first, we use an encoder to generate Gaussian distribution (z_mean, z_log_var) from input x, then, we take a sample z from this distribution, lastly, with a decoder, we reconstruct target x from z.

It is somehow similar to our previous denoising example. But instead of adding noise to input, we train the network so that these points around z_mean in latent space (with z_log_var distribution) will generate the same target x.

Let's look at the VAE sample code from pytorch examples to get a real feeling how to do it, the code is at:
https://github.com/pytorch/examples/blob/master/vae/main.py

4.3.1 pytorch VAE sample code

```
1   from __future__ import print_function
2   import argparse
3   import torch
4   import torch.utils.data
5   from torch import nn, optim
6   from torch.nn import functional as F
7   from torchvision import datasets, transforms
8   from torchvision.utils import save_image
9
10
11  parser = argparse.ArgumentParser(description='VAE MNIST Example')
12  parser.add_argument('--batch-size', type=int, default=128, metavar='N',
13                      help='input batch size for training (default: 128)')
14  parser.add_argument('--epochs', type=int, default=10, metavar='N',
15                      help='number of epochs to train (default: 10)')
16  parser.add_argument('--no-cuda', action='store_true', default=False,
17                      help='enables CUDA training')
18  parser.add_argument('--seed', type=int, default=1, metavar='S',
19                      help='random seed (default: 1)')
20  parser.add_argument('--log-interval', type=int, default=10, metavar='N',
21                      help='how many batches to wait before logging training status ←
                            ')
22  args = parser.parse_args()
23  args.cuda = not args.no_cuda and torch.cuda.is_available()
24
25  torch.manual_seed(args.seed)
26
27  device = torch.device("cuda" if args.cuda else "cpu")
28
29  kwargs = {'num_workers': 1, 'pin_memory': True} if args.cuda else {}
```

```
30  train_loader = torch.utils.data.DataLoader(
31      datasets.MNIST('../data', train=True, download=True,
32                      transform=transforms.ToTensor()),
33      batch_size=args.batch_size, shuffle=True, **kwargs)
34  test_loader = torch.utils.data.DataLoader(
35      datasets.MNIST('../data', train=False, transform=transforms.ToTensor()),
36      batch_size=args.batch_size, shuffle=True, **kwargs)
37
38
39  class VAE(nn.Module):
40      def __init__(self):
41          super(VAE, self).__init__()
42
43          self.fc1 = nn.Linear(784, 400)
44          self.fc21 = nn.Linear(400, 20)
45          self.fc22 = nn.Linear(400, 20)
46          self.fc3 = nn.Linear(20, 400)
47          self.fc4 = nn.Linear(400, 784)
48
49      def encode(self, x):
50          h1 = F.relu(self.fc1(x))
51          return self.fc21(h1), self.fc22(h1)
52
53      def reparameterize(self, mu, logvar):
54          std = torch.exp(0.5*logvar)
55          eps = torch.randn_like(std)
56          return eps.mul(std).add_(mu)
57
58      def decode(self, z):
59          h3 = F.relu(self.fc3(z))
60          return torch.sigmoid(self.fc4(h3))
61
62      def forward(self, x):
63          mu, logvar = self.encode(x.view(-1, 784))
64          z = self.reparameterize(mu, logvar)
65          return self.decode(z), mu, logvar
66
67
68  model = VAE().to(device)
69  optimizer = optim.Adam(model.parameters(), lr=1e-3)
70
71
```

```python
72   # Reconstruction + KL divergence losses summed over all elements and batch
73   def loss_function(recon_x, x, mu, logvar):
74       BCE = F.binary_cross_entropy(recon_x, x.view(-1, 784), reduction='sum')
75
76       # see Appendix B from VAE paper:
77       # Kingma and Welling. Auto-Encoding Variational Bayes. ICLR, 2014
78       # https://arxiv.org/abs/1312.6114
79       # 0.5 * sum(1 + log(sigma^2) - mu^2 - sigma^2)
80       KLD = -0.5 * torch.sum(1 + logvar - mu.pow(2) - logvar.exp())
81
82       return BCE + KLD
83
84
85   def train(epoch):
86       model.train()
87       train_loss = 0
88       for batch_idx, (data, _) in enumerate(train_loader):
89           data = data.to(device)
90           optimizer.zero_grad()
91           recon_batch, mu, logvar = model(data)
92           loss = loss_function(recon_batch, data, mu, logvar)
93           loss.backward()
94           train_loss += loss.item()
95           optimizer.step()
96           if batch_idx % args.log_interval == 0:
97               print('Train Epoch: {} [{}/{} ({:.0f}%)]\tLoss: {:.6f}'.format(
98                   epoch, batch_idx * len(data), len(train_loader.dataset),
99                   100. * batch_idx / len(train_loader),
100                  loss.item() / len(data)))
101
102      print('====> Epoch: {} Average loss: {:.4f}'.format(
103          epoch, train_loss / len(train_loader.dataset)))
104
105
106  def test(epoch):
107      model.eval()
108      test_loss = 0
109      with torch.no_grad():
110          for i, (data, _) in enumerate(test_loader):
111              data = data.to(device)
112              recon_batch, mu, logvar = model(data)
113              test_loss += loss_function(recon_batch, data, mu, logvar).item()
```

```
114            if i == 0:
115                n = min(data.size(0), 8)
116                comparison = torch.cat([data[:n],
117                                  recon_batch.view(args.batch_size, 1, 28,  ↩
                                      28)[:n]])
118                save_image(comparison.cpu(),
119                        'results/reconstruction_' + str(epoch) + '.png', nrow=n)
120
121    test_loss /= len(test_loader.dataset)
122    print('====> Test set loss: {:.4f}'.format(test_loss))
123
124 if __name__ == "__main__":
125     for epoch in range(1, args.epochs + 1):
126         train(epoch)
127         test(epoch)
128         with torch.no_grad():
129             sample = torch.randn(64, 20).to(device)
130             sample = model.decode(sample).cpu()
131             save_image(sample.view(64, 1, 28, 28),
132                     'results/sample_' + str(epoch) + '.png')
```

4.3.2   pytorch VAE sample code analysis

We can read from the middle of the code in order to understand it better.

- Line 30-36, load MNIST data.

- Line 39-65, define a VAE model.
  If we remember the previous denoising autoencoder, it is quite similar.
  First, we encode an input into a 2-d latent space (mu, logvar) in Line 63. Then, we add some noise/resampling from this 2-d feature space using a Gaussian distribution defined in Line 53-56. Finally, we use that information to the decoder to reconstruct the original input.
  Some neural network magic here. If we intercept those outputs from the encoder as z_mean, and z_log_var, then the network will generate/train those two things for us. Magic? Get it?

- Line 73 - 82 defined a loss function for VAE, which is BCE + KL loss.
  The BCE loss can be thought of as reconstruct loss, where the KL loss refer to Kullback–Leibler divergence (also called relative entropy), which is a measure of how one probability distribution is different from a second, reference probability distribution.
  https://stats.stackexchange.com/questions/7440/kl-divergence-between-two-univariate-gaussians showed how to

calculate the KL diverge between two univariate Gaussians.

In this case, for each point in latent space, we use KL loss to measure how far off the distribution we are training is away from a standard normal distribution.

The intuition behind it is:

we want to encourage the encoder to distribute encodings with normal distribution around the center of its target in the latent space.

- Line 85 - 100 defined a pretty standard pytorch training process.

- Line 106 - 122 visualized a reconstruction on a test data.

- Line 124 - 132, showed we can we randomly sample from latent space, reconstruct some digits.

4.3.3   VAE running results

Let's run it:

```
(pytorch_env) vae$ python main.py
...
...
Processing...
Done!
Train Epoch: 1 [0/60000 (0%)]    Loss: 550.187805
Train Epoch: 1 [1280/60000 (2%)]         Loss: 323.104736
Train Epoch: 1 [2560/60000 (4%)]         Loss: 237.460968
Train Epoch: 1 [3840/60000 (6%)]         Loss: 216.792160
Train Epoch: 1 [5120/60000 (9%)]         Loss: 205.568695
...
...
Train Epoch: 1 [55040/60000 (92%)]       Loss: 130.176987
Train Epoch: 1 [56320/60000 (94%)]       Loss: 126.856277
Train Epoch: 1 [57600/60000 (96%)]       Loss: 132.204620
Train Epoch: 1 [58880/60000 (98%)]       Loss: 130.612930
====> Epoch: 1 Average loss: 164.1694

====> Test set loss: 105.9475
Train Epoch: 10 [0/60000 (0%)]   Loss: 106.763062
Train Epoch: 10 [1280/600000 (2%)]        Loss: 109.533699
Train Epoch: 10 [2560/60000 (4%)]         Loss: 103.380898
...
```

```
24   ...
25   Train Epoch: 10 [56320/60000 (94%)]      Loss: 103.473251
26   Train Epoch: 10 [57600/60000 (96%)]      Loss: 101.515335
27   Train Epoch: 10 [58880/60000 (98%)]      Loss: 107.964027
28   ====> Epoch: 10 Average loss: 106.1417
29   ====> Test set loss: 105.7168
```

It will generate some graphs under the directory of results/:

```
1   ls results/
2   reconstruction_10.png   reconstruction_3.png   reconstruction_6.png
3   reconstruction_9.png   sample_2.png   sample_5.png   sample_8.png
4   reconstruction_1.png    reconstruction_4.png   reconstruction_7.png
5   sample_10.png           sample_3.png   sample_6.png   sample_9.png
6   reconstruction_2.png    reconstruction_5.png   reconstruction_8.png
7   sample_1.png            sample_4.png   sample_7.png
```

The following figure showed the original input image and the reconstructed output image :

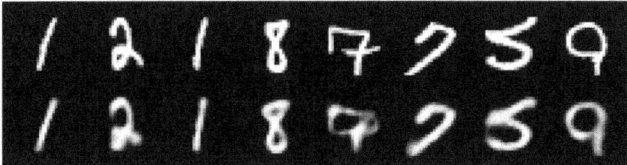

Figure 4.5: VAE original input and reconstructed output

Here are images generated from auto-encoder by sampling from latent space:

Figure 4.6: VAE sample from latent space and reconstructed output

In general, we can sample any point from the latent space, then generate new data, thus, VAE is called a **generative model**.

There is no limit to what you can generate! Can we create new interesting movies, music songs this way in the future? You bet!

4.4   summary

In this chapter, we learned our first un-supervised/self-supervised learning method: autoencoder.

Another similar, but more general, technique, called **GAN (generative adversarial network)**, uses a generator and a discriminator to capture the training data's distribution, so that we can generate new data from that same distribution.

Since pytorch provided an excellent tutorial at:
https://pytorch.org/tutorials/beginner/dcgan_faces_tutorial.html ,
I will skip GAN in this book.

So far, after reading this chapter, you should be able to:

- construct an autoencoder for data denoising.

- understand VAE and apply VAE to some interesting projects.

Chapter 5

Deep reinforcement learning

Reinforcement learning (RL) is another interesting machine learning technique. It does NOT require an explicit pair of (data, labels), but needs some numeric indication of "how good a sample is", e.g: a score in a video game. Thus, RL is neither a purely supervised learning nor pure unsupervised learning. It is a new way of learning.

Quote from Wikipedia:

```
1  Reinforcement learning (RL) is an area of machine learning,
2  concerned with how software agents ought to take actions
3  in an environment so as to maximize some notion of cumulative reward.
```

The following diagram shows a general reinforcement learning architecture.

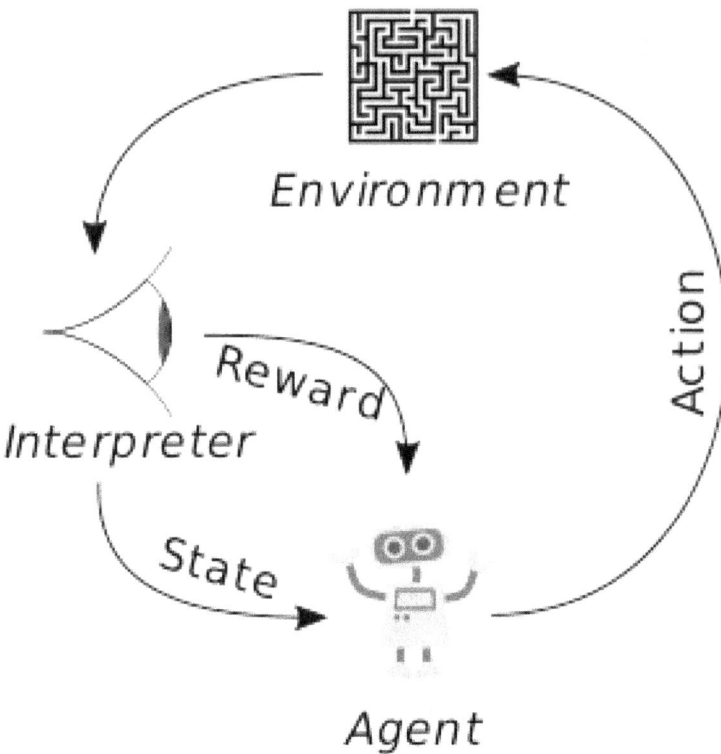

Figure 5.1: Reinforcement learning architecture

As shown in the picture, an **agent** takes **actions** in an environment, after each action, the agent receives a **feedback** which consists of the **reward** and next **state** of the environment.

The goal in RL is generally learning how to map observations and measurements to a set of actions while trying to maximize some long-term rewards.

Thus, RL allows us to create an AI agent that can learn from the environment by interacting with it mainly through feedback. It learns everything on its own from data collection to model evaluation. After a lot of trial and error, it will have enough experience to succeed in that environment.

A recent trend is to apply a deep neural network to RL areas, the combination of RL and deep learning is called **deep reinforcement learning (deep RL)**. It can solve a wide range of complex decision-making tasks that could not be solved before.

Some people call deep RL **end-to-end reinforcement learning** to emphasizes that the entire end-to-end process is trained by RL without explicitly designing the state/action space. Google's deepmind applied this approach very successfully to Atari/AlphaGo games (will be covered in the next chapter).

Deep RL opens up many new applications domains, for example,

- Computer games such as Atari, board game Go, etc.
  The most successful example is AlphaGo which uses reinforcement learning to learn about its next move based on the current board position.

- Robot control, industrial automation.
  Using reinforcement learning, robots can learn to walk, run, dance, fly, play ping pong or stack Legos, etc.

- Media and online advertising.
  A computer program can use RL to select an ad to show to a user at the right time, or in the right format.

- Education and training.
  RL can enable tutoring systems to provide custom instruction and materials tuned to the needs of individual students.

- Health and medicine.
  Many researchers use RL to find optimal treatment policies in health care, etc.

Excited about deep RL?

In this chapter, we will explore Q-learning and its different variants, a popular RL technique often found in computer games. By digging into the sample code, you should be able to understand how deep RL really works.

Let's start.

5.1 Q-learning

Q-learning is one of the popular reinforcement learning techniques. Its goal is to learn a policy to get best result/score. The policy essentially tells an agent how to act under certain circumstances.

To be more specific, let's say we have a RL system:

- an agent

- a set of states: { S } (state space)

- a set of actions: { A } (action space)

The agent transitions from state to state by performing an action in { A }. A reward (a numerical score) is given when the agent executes an action in a specific state. The reward is usually pre-defined by some means.

In Q-learning, the goal of the agent is to take a specific action from the current state in such a way that it will maximize its total (future) reward. The total future reward is a weighted sum of the expected values of the rewards of all future steps starting from the current state.

Pause it for a moment, please notice it is a total sum of future rewards, not just the immediate reward by executing an action in a specific state. You will see it more clearly later when we introduce some math notation

This total reward (often called **Q-score**) can be said to stand for the quality of an action taken in a given state.

If we know Q-score of each action at every state (in other word we already found the best policy) , choosing the next action becomes easy: we simply choose an action with the highest Q-score.

Now, we reduced an RL learning to a more specific one: find a good way to assign accurate Q-scores to different actions under a certain state. As the process is mainly about finding accurate Q-scores, thus, it is called Q-learning.

Tip
Note these Q scores have no meaning outside the context of their simulation/context. They have no absolute significance as they are just for comparisons.

We need some math here to get a more accurate understanding of Q-score.

Let's use $Q(S_t,a)$ function to denote the expected future reward (Q score) of taking action a at state s at step/time t. Mathematically it can be expressed as :

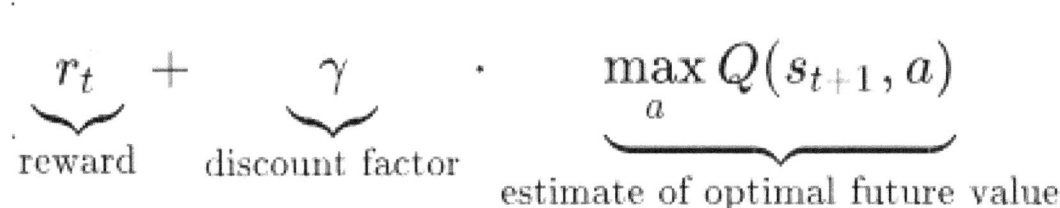

$$\underbrace{r_t}_{\text{reward}} + \underbrace{\gamma}_{\text{discount factor}} \cdot \underbrace{\max_a Q(s_{t+1}, a)}_{\text{estimate of optimal future value}}$$

Figure 5.2: Q score at S(t) for action a

Where reward in the figure above means reward received when moving from state S(t) to new state S(t+1).

As you can see, Q(S(t),a) depends on its future (next step) score Q(S(t+1)), it is sort of **recursive** into the future.

So how do we know Q(S(t+1))?

Well, it turned out that we can learn it **by simulation play or self-play**. Our computation power brings insights to the future!

Before deep learning, Q can be trained and updated according to the following formula:

$$Q^{new}(s_t, a_t) \leftarrow (1-\alpha) \cdot \underbrace{Q(s_t, a_t)}_{\text{old value}} + \underbrace{\alpha}_{\text{learning rate}} \cdot \left(\underbrace{r_t}_{\text{reward}} + \underbrace{\gamma}_{\text{discount factor}} \cdot \overbrace{\underbrace{\max_a Q(s_{t+1}, a)}_{\text{estimate of optimal future value}}}^{\text{learned value}} \right)$$

Figure 5.3: Q score training/update procedure

I will skip explaining those items above as this book is focused on deep DL, and most of the items are self-explained. Interesting readers can read more details at:

https://en.wikipedia.org/wiki/Q-learning

With deep learning, it could be greatly simplified.

We just need to set up a DNN as our policy network, which can predict a Q-score Q(s,a) based on the state s and action a.

Then we defined a loss function like below for this policy DNN.

$$loss = \left(r + \gamma \max_{a`} \hat{Q}(s, a`) - Q(s, a) \right)^2$$

Reward — Decay Rate — Target — Prediction

Figure 5.4: loss function for Q-learning in DNN

By collecting and feeding target value into the DNN, the DNN can learn what is the best policy.

Remember, the target value can be collected by **by simulation play or self-play**.

We will look at this in more detail in the next section.

5.2 Deep Q-learning (DQN)

In 2013, Google's DeepMind published its famous paper "Playing Atari with Deep Reinforcement Learning" at:
https://arxiv.org/abs/1312.5602

They introduced a new algorithm called **Deep Q Network (DQN)**. It demonstrated how an AI agent can learn to play games by just observing the screen with no prior information about those games. The result turned out to be pretty impressive. They can play Atari 2600 games at expert human levels! This paper opened the era of **deep reinforcement learning**.

You may wonder: what make DQN unique? What kind of problems have been solved?

Quote from another famous paper "Human-level control through deep reinforcement learning":

```
1  Reinforcement learning is known to be unstable or
2  even to diverge when a nonlinear function approximator
```

```
3    such as a neural network is used to represent the action-value
4    (also known as Q) function. This instability has several causes:
5    the correlations present in the sequence of observations,
6    the fact that small updates to Q may significantly change the policy
7    and therefore change the data distribution,
8    and the correlations between the action-values and the target values.
9
10   We address these instabilities with a novel variant of Q-learning,
11   which uses two key ideas. First, we used a biologically inspired
12   mechanism termed experience replay that randomizes over the data,
13   thereby removing correlations in the observation sequence
14   and smoothing over changes in the data distribution.
15   Second, we used an iterative update that adjusts the action-values (Q)
16   towards target values that are only periodically updated,
17   thereby reducing correlations with the target.
```

Similar to Q-learning, Deep Q-learning just uses a neural network to approximate the reward based on the state.

The key techniques in DQN are **experience replay** and **iterative update**, which are aimed to solve the instability issue.

Interesting readers can find more details at:

https://www.nature.com/articles/nature14236

https://web.stanford.edu/class/psych209/Readings/MnihEtAlHassibis15NatureControlDeepRL.pdf

It is better to use a simple example to illustrate how deep Q-learning works.

In the following sections: * first, I will introduce you a simple game under OpenAI Gym environment,

- then I will show you the sample code of DQN, and

- finally, I will do the code analysis to help you understand the DQN.

5.2.1   OpenAI Gym environment, a sample game: cartpole-v0

OpenAI Gym is a toolkit/simulator for developing and comparing reinforcement learning algorithms.

The Gym environments have two main parts: an observation space and action space.

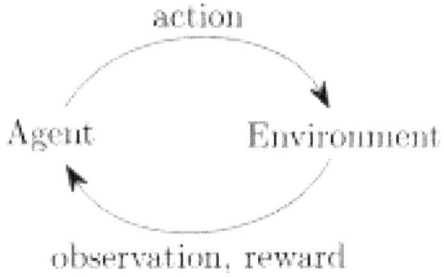

Figure 5.5: openai gym

As shown in the above figure, an agent observes something in observation space from the environment, that info will be used by that agent to determine what is the best next action.

One good thing about OpenAI gym environment is it provides a very straightforward way of gathering data: we can essentially just run through the simulation many times, and take random steps/actions.

Let's start from a Gym game called **CartPole**. It is one of the simplest environments in OpenAI gym.

Quote from: https://gym.openai.com/envs/CartPole-v0/

```
A pole is attached by an un-actuated joint to a cart,
which moves along a frictionless track.
The system is controlled by applying a force of +1 or -1 to the cart.
The pendulum starts upright, and the goal is to prevent it from falling over.
A reward of +1 is provided for every timestep that the pole remains upright.
The episode ends when the pole is more than 15 degrees from vertical,
or the cart moves more than 2.4 units from the center.
```

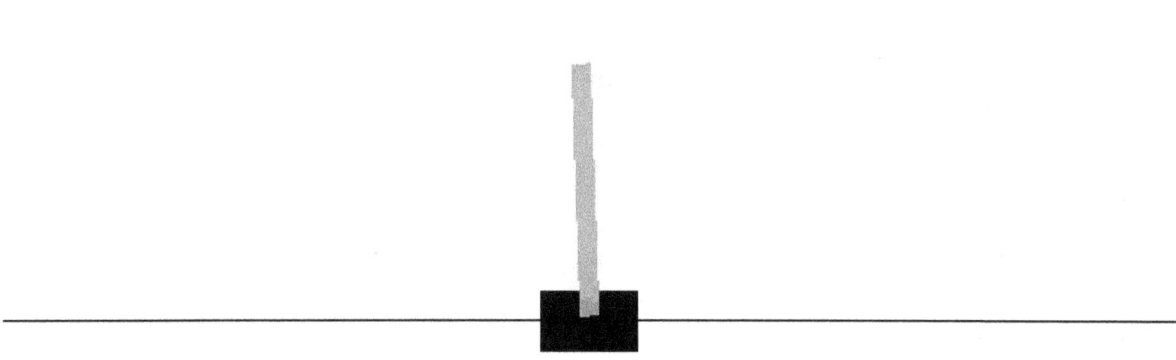

Figure 5.6: cartpole game, the goal is to prevent the pole from falling over

Gym makes interacting with the game environment really simple.

For example, in this CartPole game, Gym provides:

- a state of the game, e.g.: angle of the pole and position of the cart etc.

- actions such as +1, -1 to indicate if we want to move left or right.

- at a certain state, we apply an action to the game by using step function provided by the Gym simulator:
  next_state, reward, done, info = env.step(action)
  Then the game will move to next_state, and we will get a reward score for this action.

- done is a Boolean value telling whether the game ended or not.

Of course, some additional info could be passed to us depending on the game.

CartPole-v0 defines "solving" as getting an average reward of 195.0 over 100 consecutive trials.

Let's explore the game using python:

```
1   # install gym first
2   # "sudo pip3 install gym" should work on most platforms.
3   # we will explore gym here
4
5   >>> import gym
6   >>> import numpy as np
7
8   # load CartPole-v0 game
9   >>> env = gym.make("CartPole-v0")
10
11  # observation is a record of current state
12  >>> observation = env.reset()
13  >>> observation
14  # [position of cart, velocity of cart, angle of pole, rotation rate of pole]
15  #https://github.com/openai/gym/blob/master/gym/envs/classic_control/cartpole.py# ↩
        L75
16  array([ 0.00771999,  0.02024324, -0.03827106,  0.00847261])
17
18  #  For this game, the only have two actions, left or right
19  >>> action = np.random.randint(0, 2)
20
21  # now apply the action on the environment, then get the feedback
22  >>> observation, reward, done, _ = env.step(action)
23
24  >>> observation
25  array([ 0.00812486, -0.17430955, -0.03810161,  0.28883915])
26  >>> reward
27  1.0
28  >>> done
29  False
30
31  # this is action space dimension
32  >>> print(env.action_space)
33  Discrete(2)
34
35  # observation_space dimension
36  >>> print(env.observation_space)
37  Box(4,)
```

You can find more information at:

https://gym.openai.com/docs

https://github.com/openai/gym/wiki/Leaderboard

5.2.2   DQN for cartpole-v0 (source code)

Now, we know what cartople game about, how can we use DQN to play this game? In other words, how can we find a strategy to play this game so that we could get an average reward of 195.0 over 100 consecutive trials?

Pytorch official site provides a tutorial at:
https://pytorch.org/tutorials/intermediate/reinforcement_q_learning.html

The code is at:
https://github.com/pytorch/tutorials/blob/master/intermediate_source/reinforcement_q_learning.py

However, the training code does not converge!! But the article is still worth to to be read.

The following DQN code converges, and showed you how to train and play this game.

The code is long, but worth to read it as code is the most accurate documentation!

Tip
You can download the complete code of this example from the author's repo
(https://github.com/mingewang/pytorch_deep_learning_by_example) **at:**
reinforcement/pytorch_dqn_cartpole.py

There are many comments inside the code to help you understand it. Also, I've put a code analysis after that to further highlight what needs to be understood.

```
1   #
2   # Pytorch Deep Q-learning for Gym's game
3   # Min Wang <mingewang@gmail.com>
4   #
5   import argparse
6   import gym
7   import random
8   import numpy as np
9   # list-like container with fast appends and pops on either end
10  from collections import deque
11
12  import math
```

```python
13  import matplotlib
14  import matplotlib.pyplot as plt
15
16  import torch
17  import torch.nn as nn
18  import torch.optim as optim
19  import torch.nn.functional as F
20  import torchvision.transforms as T
21
22  # if gpu is to be used
23  device = torch.device("cuda" if torch.cuda.is_available() else "cpu")
24
25  class DQN_module(nn.Module):
26      # env.state_size, output_dim = env.action_space.n
27      def __init__(self, input_dim, output_dim):
28          super(DQN_module, self).__init__()
29          self.l1 = nn.Linear(input_dim, 24)
30          self.l2 = nn.Linear(24,24)
31          self.l3 = nn.Linear(24,output_dim)
32
33      def forward(self, x):
34          #import pdb; pdb.set_trace()
35          x = F.relu(self.l1(x))
36          x = F.relu(self.l2(x))
37          x = self.l3(x)
38          return x
39
40  class DQN:
41      def __init__(self, env, load_model):
42          self.env      = env
43          self.load_model      = load_model
44          # we save weights here
45          self.weights_filename = "dqn_success.model"
46
47          # observation space dimension
48          self.state_size  = env.observation_space.shape[0]
49          # action space dimension
50          self.predict_size = self.env.action_space.n
51
52          # The Experience Replay buffer stores a fixed number of recent memories
53          # and as new ones come in, old ones are removed.
54          # When the time comes to train, we simply draw a uniform batch
```

```
55          # of random memories from the buffer, and train our network with them.
56          self.memory   = deque(maxlen=2000)
57
58          # hyper parameters for DQN
59          self.learning_rate = 0.005
60          # discount factor for DQN
61          self.gamma = 0.99
62          # start with 1 but will decay for each action
63          self.epsilon = 1.0
64          self.epsilon_min = 0.01
65          self.epsilon_decay = 0.999 #0.995
66
67          # minimum sample pool
68          self.train_start = 1000
69
70          # we use batch training to add more stability for the learning process
71          self.batch_size = 64
72
73          # how do we want to load weights for target model from model's weights
74          self.tau = 1
75
76          # our output/predict is: reward for each action
77          # here we only have two actions: left, right
78          # the target = model.predict(state)
79          # is: target[0][0]= reward0
80          #     target[0][1]= reward1
81          # the first index 0 is for index for the data
82          # if we feed an array of data to predict
83          # it will output an array of predictions for those data
84          self.model        = DQN_module( self.state_size, self.predict_size).to( ↵
                device)
85          self.target_model = DQN_module( self.state_size, self.predict_size).to( ↵
                device)
86
87          self.criterion = torch.nn.MSELoss()
88          self.optimizer = optim.Adam(self.model.parameters(), lr=self. ↵
                learning_rate)
89
90          if self.load_model:
91            self.model.load_state_dict( torch.load(self.weights_filename) );
92
93      def act(self, state):
```

```
94          # will be smaller,smaller as we learned
95          self.epsilon *= self.epsilon_decay
96          self.epsilon = max(self.epsilon_min, self.epsilon)
97          if random.random() < self.epsilon:
98              # return some random action to explore environment
99              return torch.tensor( self.env.action_space.sample() )
100         # choose an action which has the max reward based on our model prediction
101         return torch.argmax(self.model(state)[0])
102
103     def demo_act(self, state):
104         # choose an action which has the max reward based on our model prediction
105         return torch.argmax(self.model(state)[0])
106
107     def remember(self, state, action, reward, new_state, done):
108         self.memory.append([state, action, reward, new_state, done])
109
110     # major Google DeepMind contribution as DQN
111     def replay(self):
112         # do not have many samples, do not replay
113         if len(self.memory) < self.train_start:
114             return
115
116         # enter train mode
117         self.model.train()
118         self.target_model.eval()
119
120         # we use batch training, initial buffer here
121         trainning_input = torch.zeros((self.batch_size, self.state_size))
122         trainning_target = torch.zeros((self.batch_size, self.predict_size ))
123         trainning_pred = torch.zeros((self.batch_size, self.predict_size ))
124
125         # Experience Replay,
126         # choose random samples from our storage
127         samples = random.sample(self.memory, self.batch_size)
128
129         for idx, sample in enumerate(samples):
130             state, action, reward, new_state, done = sample
131             # our model predicts what reward on those actions
132             # based on current state
133             # the target should be:
134             # target[0][action0] -> reward0
135             # target[0][action1] -> reward1
```

```
136              # ...
137              my_predict = self.model(state)
138              # store my_predict as model's predict
139              trainning_pred[idx] = my_predict
140
141              my_next_predict = self.model(new_state)
142              # target model prediction for next new_state
143              target = self.target_model(new_state)
144
145              if done:
146                  my_predict[0][action] = reward
147              else:
148                  # key point of dqn
149                  # choose action use target model's prediction
150                  a =  torch.argmax( target )
151                  # but use reward from target model using that action
152                  Q_future = target[0][a]
153                  # update predict training data
154                  my_predict[0][action] = reward + Q_future * self.gamma
155
156              # store our training data: state->predict
157              trainning_input[idx] = state
158              # assume to be our ground truth
159              trainning_target[idx] = my_predict
160
161          # use NN to do the batch_size training
162          loss = self.criterion( trainning_pred,  trainning_target )
163          self.optimizer.zero_grad()
164          loss.backward()
165          self.optimizer.step()
166
167      # train target network
168      # here we just load weights from model
169      def target_train(self):
170          self.target_model.load_state_dict(self.model.state_dict())
171
172      def save_model(self):
173          torch.save( self.model.state_dict(), self.weights_filename )
174
175  def train():
176      # load the game
177      env      = gym.make("CartPole-v0")
```

```
178
179     # how many trials we want to play the game
180     trials  = 10000
181     # how deep we want
182     max_trial_step = 500
183     # CartPole-v0 defines "solving" as getting average reward of 195.0
184     # over 100 consecutive trials.
185     # to speed up, we check avg of last 10 scores
186     scores  = deque(maxlen=10)
187     target_score = 195
188
189     # if game finish earlier, we give a penalty score
190     penaty_score = 100
191     max_score = 200
192
193     training_ok = False
194
195     dqn_agent = DQN(env=env, load_model=False)
196
197     # how many times we want to play
198     for trial in range(trials):
199         # reset the env for each episode play
200         cur_state = torch.from_numpy( env.reset().reshape(1, dqn_agent.state_size ←
                ) ).float()
201         score = 0
202         # for each play, how deep/how many steps do we want to play
203         for step in range(max_trial_step):
204             # render game
205             # env.render()
206             # action based on our model's prediction
207             #import pdb; pdb.set_trace()
208             action = dqn_agent.act(cur_state)
209             #print( cur_state, action)
210
211             # use gym simulator to go the next step, env take numpy instead of ←
                    tensor
212             new_state, reward, done, _ = env.step( action.numpy() )
213             #print( done, new_state, reward, action)
214
215             new_state = torch.from_numpy( new_state.reshape(1,dqn_agent. ←
                state_size) ).float()
216
```

```
217            # if an action make the episode end, then gives penalty
218            # we want this as long as possible
219            reward = reward if not done or score == max_score else -penaty_score
220
221            # store play steps
222            dqn_agent.remember(cur_state, action, reward, new_state, done)
223
224            # try to train in every step
225            dqn_agent.replay()
226
227            # in this case, score is just  + 1
228            score +=  reward
229            cur_state = new_state
230
231            if done:
232                # iterates target model
233                dqn_agent.target_train()
234                # revert back to see avg score
235                score = score if score == max_score else score + penaty_score
236                break
237
238        scores.append( score )
239        avg_score = np.mean(scores)
240        print("Episode {}# Score: {}, avg score: {}, ".format(trial, score,  ↩
               avg_score))
241
242        if avg_score > target_score:
243          dqn_agent.save_model()
244          training_ok = True
245          break
246
247    if training_ok:
248      print(" avg score above target score , training OK!")
249    else:
250      print("Failed to train the model after trials:", trials)
251
252 def demo():
253     env      = gym.make("CartPole-v0")
254
255     trials  = 20
256     max_trial_step = 500
257
```

```python
258        dqn_agent = DQN(env=env, load_model=True)
259
260        # how many times we want to play
261        for trial in range(trials):
262            cur_state = torch.from_numpy( env.reset().reshape(1, dqn_agent.state_size ↩
                   ) ).float()
263            score = 0
264            # for each play, how deep/how many steps do we want to play
265            for step in range(max_trial_step):
266                # render
267                env.render()
268                # based on our model's prediction, we choose max reward one
269                action = dqn_agent.demo_act(cur_state)
270                # use simulator to go the next step
271                new_state, reward, done, _ = env.step(action.numpy())
272                new_state = torch.from_numpy( new_state.reshape(1,dqn_agent. ↩
                       state_size) ).float()
273                # in this case, score is just  + 1
274                score +=  reward
275                cur_state = new_state
276
277                if done:
278                    break
279
280            print("Demo mode, Episode {}# Score: {}".format(trial, score))
281
282
283    if __name__ == "__main__":
284        parser = argparse.ArgumentParser(description='Demo')
285        parser.add_argument('--demo',
286                action='store_true',
287                help='demo flag' )
288
289        args = parser.parse_args()
290
291        if args.demo:
292            demo()
293
294        else:
295            train()
```

5.2.3   Code analysis: DQN for cartpole-v0

Here are some highlights of DQN's key points to help you understand the code better.

5.2.3.1   deep learning model for DQN

One major addition to DQN from Google is it uses a deep NN to do the Q-learning.

- Line 25-38 defined a neural network model. How to design/choose a DNN model depends on the nature of the problem. For this simple cartpole game, a simple 3-layer NN is used.

- Line 59-74 defined some hyper parameters for DQN.

  - learning_rate - Determines how much neural net learns in each iteration.

  - gamma - aka decay or discount rate, to calculate the future discounted reward.

  - epsilon - aka exploration rate, this is the rate in which an agent randomly decides its action rather than prediction.

  - epsilon_decay - we want to decrease the number of explorations as it gets good at playing games.

  - epsilon_min - we want the agent to explore at least this amount.

5.2.3.2   experience replay

- Line 56, showed another major addition to DQN from Google Deepmind.
  The basic idea is that by storing an agent's experiences, and then randomly drawing batches of them to train the network, we can more robustly learn to perform well in the task. This strategy can prevent the network from only learning about what it is immediately doing in the environment, and allow it to learn from a more varied array of past experiences.
  Each of these experiences is stored as a tuple of <state,action,reward,next state>. The Experience Replay buffer stores a fixed number of recent memories, and as new ones come in, old ones are removed. When the time comes to train, we simply draw a uniform batch of random memories from the buffer, and train our network with them.

5.2.3.3   two separate models (Separate target network)

- Line 84-85, two models are created. That is the third major addition from google's DQN.
  This technique was introduced to stabilize the training process.
  This second network (target model) is used to generate the target-Q values that will be used to compute the loss for every action during training.

- Line 145 - 154 shows how Q value is generated for the training data set.
  Why do we need that? Why not just use one network for both estimations?
  The issue is that at every step of training, the Q-network's values shift, and if we are using a constantly shifting set of values to adjust our network values, then the value estimations can easily spiral out of control. The network can become destabilized by falling into feedback loops between the target and estimated Q-values.
  In order to mitigate that risk, the target network's weights are fixed, and only periodically or slowly updated to the primary Q-networks values. In this way, training can proceed in a more stable manner.

- Line 169-170 shows how to update our target model.
  The self.tau parameter could give us another flexibility to adjust the target model.
  In this game, we just set self.tau = 1, so what we actually do is just update target model's weights with the model's weights.

5.2.3.4 how to pick the next action

- Line 93 - 101 showed how we pick up the next action.
  We do this as commented in the code is to allow the code to explore environment.
  Initially, we have no idea what the environment looks like, so we just randomly choose some actions to explore at first by a certain percentage called 'exploration rate' or 'epsilon'.
  This is because at first, it is better for the agent to try all kinds of things before it starts to see the patterns.
  As time goes by, we get more familiar with the environment, we begin to based on our previous experience/data to choose the next action.
  In this game, the agent will predict the reward value based on the current state and pick the action that will give the highest reward.

- Line 101 should read like this as two lines as following:

  – action = self.model.predict(state)

  – torch.argmax(action[0])

    Where acttion[0] looks like this: [0.67, 0.2], each numbers representing the reward of picking action 0 and 1. And torch.argmax() is the function that picks the highest value between two elements in the actions[0]. In the example of [0.67, 0.2], argmax returns 0 because the value in the 0th index is the highest.

5.2.3.5 how it really learned

- Line 111 -165 shows how QDN learns.
  We will use mini-batches with batch_size=64 instead of 1 (online learning/Stochastic learning) to learn. It gives us benefits of not only fast weights update (than whole data set), but a more accurate estimate of the gradient for each propagation (than stochastic learning).

  I found this is important, as my previous code was batch_size=1, the result is quite unstable, and not easy to converge. The reason is: trident changes its direction was far more often than a mini-batch.

- Line 143 is the prediction from our model if we are in the next_state. The target looks like :

  - target[0][action0] = reward0
  - target[0][action1] = reward1

- Line 150 - 154 is the key point of this DQN.

- Line 150 choose the next action based on the max rewards predicted by our target_model.

- Line 152 is the reward predicted from our target_model.

- Line 154 calculated the Q reward we suppose to get:
  Q(state) = reward + gamma * Q(next_state)
  target = reward + gamma * torch.amax(model.predict(next_state))
  This Q is supposed to be our prediction from the current model.

- Line 157-159 just fills up training data and target value.

- Line 162-65 is a pytorch standard process to train the data.

5.2.3.6 how it is trained

- Line 157 - 250 are the main code block which showed how we play the game, store the games, and train the model. Most of the code should be self-explained.

- Line 219 is worth noting. We give penalty if the episode is done as our goal is to let the cartpole stay as long as it could.

I hope with the help of such detailed comments, you have no trouble to understand RL and DQN.

5.2.3.7 run and demo

Ok, time to run the code:

```
(pytorch_env) $ python ./pytorch_dqn_cartpole.py
Episode 0# Score: 24.0, avg score: 24.0,
Episode 1# Score: 13.0, avg score: 18.5,
Episode 2# Score: 31.0, avg score: 22.666666666666668,
Episode 3# Score: 15.0, avg score: 20.75,
Episode 4# Score: 13.0, avg score: 19.2,
Episode 5# Score: 27.0, avg score: 20.5,
...
...
Episode 114# Score: 161.0, avg score: 144.8,
Episode 115# Score: 199.0, avg score: 154.8,
Episode 116# Score: 199.0, avg score: 161.3,
Episode 117# Score: 199.0, avg score: 161.3,
Episode 118# Score: 199.0, avg score: 170.7,
Episode 119# Score: 199.0, avg score: 179.1,
Episode 120# Score: 172.0, avg score: 181.7,
Episode 121# Score: 199.0, avg score: 187.1,
Episode 122# Score: 199.0, avg score: 187.2,
Episode 123# Score: 199.0, avg score: 192.5,
Episode 124# Score: 199.0, avg score: 196.3,
 avg score above target score , training OK!
```

As we can see, after about 124 times ran, we get an average score above 195 for the last 10 episodes.

After the training, we can see how the game was played by running the code in demo mode:

```
python ./pytorch_dqn_cartpole_2.py  --demo
```

5.3 Double Q-learning (DDQN)

Because the maximum approximated action value is used in Q-learning, in noisy environments, Q-learning can sometimes overestimate the action values, thus, slow the learning.

A variant called Double Q-learning was proposed to correct this. This algorithm was later combined with deep learning, as in the DQN algorithm, resulting in **Double DQN (DDQN)**, which outperforms the original DQN algorithm.

The original paper claims:

```
1  Double DQN appears more robust to this more challenging evaluation,
2  suggesting that appropriate generalizations
3  occur and that the found solutions do not exploit
4  the determinism of the environment.
5  This is appealing, as it indicates progress towards
6  finding general solutions rather than
7  a deterministic sequence of steps that would be less robust.
```

More details could be found at:+ https://arxiv.org/abs/1509.06461

What is the difference between DQN and DDQN?

A code sample of DDQN will easily show the difference between DQN and DDQN.

5.3.1   DDQN implementation for cartpole (source code)

You can download the complete code of this example from the author's repo (https://github.com/mingewang/pytorch_deep_learning_by_example) at: reinforcement/pytorch_ddqn_cartpole.py

5.3.2   DDQN and DQN source code difference

The only difference between DQN and DDQN is at:
* Line 148-154, here we use action predicted from the model (different from DQN which use predicted action from target_model), but use the same reward from its associated action from target_model as DQN.

5.3.3   DDQN running results

```
1  (pytorch_env) $ python pytorch_ddqn_cartpole.py
2  Episode 0# Score: 29.0, avg score: 29.0,
3  Episode 1# Score: 33.0, avg score: 31.0,
```

```
4   Episode 2# Score: 27.0, avg score: 29.666666666666668,
5   Episode 3# Score: 28.0, avg score: 29.25,
6   Episode 4# Score: 17.0, avg score: 26.8,
7   Episode 5# Score: 15.0, avg score: 24.833333333333332,
8   ...
9   ...
10  Episode 87# Score: 199.0, avg score: 155.5,
11  Episode 88# Score: 173.0, avg score: 164.3,
12  Episode 89# Score: 199.0, avg score: 171.6,
13  Episode 90# Score: 199.0, avg score: 173.9,
14  Episode 91# Score: 199.0, avg score: 180.0,
15  Episode 92# Score: 199.0, avg score: 183.3,
16  Episode 93# Score: 199.0, avg score: 187.0,
17  Episode 94# Score: 199.0, avg score: 192.4,
18  Episode 95# Score: 199.0, avg score: 196.4,
19   avg score above target score , training OK!
```

It showed that DDQN did show some improvement, we just need to train 95 episodes to get similar performance as DQN.

Interesting readers could find more use cases where DDQN shines at:
https://arxiv.org/abs/1509.06461

5.4 summary

After reading this chapter, you should be able to:

- understand what is Q-learning, what is Q-score and how it is defined.

- play games in the OpenAI Gym environment.

- understand what is DQN/DDQN, and how they are trained.

Chapter 6

Learning from scratch (self-play) AlphaZero

An acute reader may notice, from previous reinforcement learning chapter, that we need some reward functions (DQN, DDQN, etc) for each action at each state in the OpenAI Gym simulator That is quite demanding!

Many real-life games such as. Chess, go etc. do not have the reward function at each step/state, we only know the result at the end of the game, either winning or losing.

How can we address those issues?

The innovative paper "Mastering the Game of Go without Human Knowledge" unveiled a new variant of the algorithm called **AlphaGo Zero** to solve such problems!

The AlphaGo Zero utilized deep CNN network and RL. Incredibly, starting from blank state (zero or scratch), solely through self-play, it gradually finds strategies to beat previous incarnations of itself with no human knowledge!

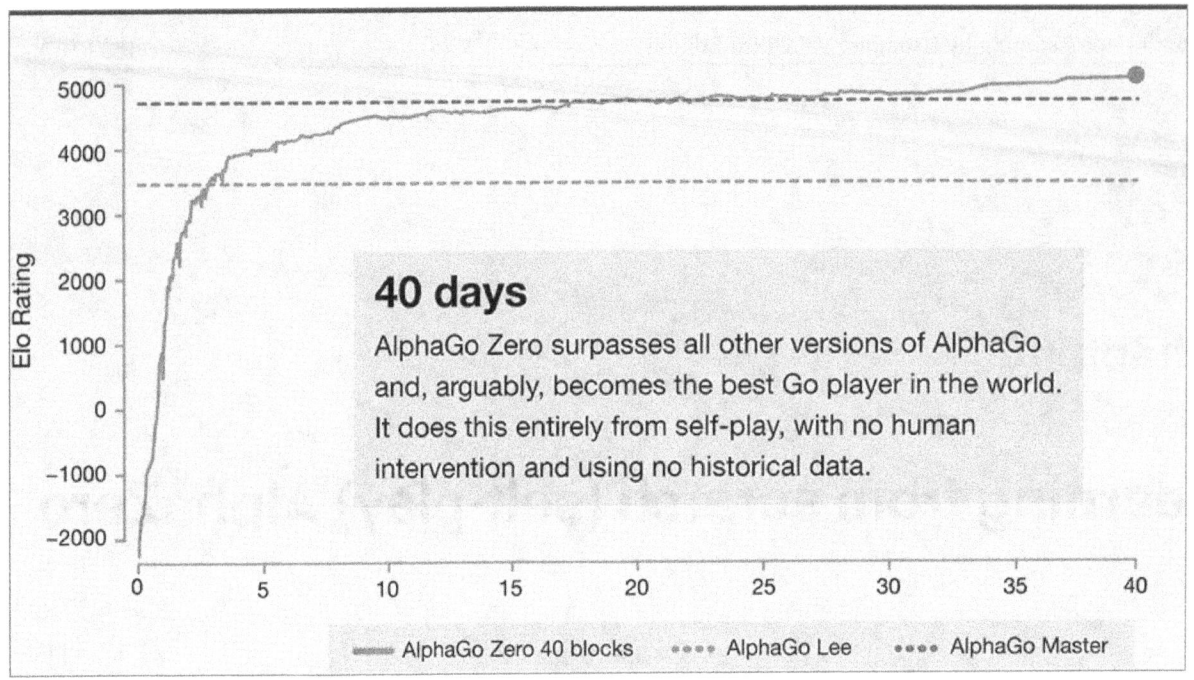

Figure 6.1: how fast AlphaGo Zero learned

The above graph showed how fast AlphaGo Zero learned.

Google later (Dec 2017) developed a generalized version of AlphaGo Zero called **AlphaZero**, that could play chess and Shōgi in addition to Go.

It cannot be overstated how important alphazero is. The underlying methodology of AlphaZero can be applied to any game with perfect information (the game state is fully known to both players at all times) because no prior expertise is required beyond the rules of the game.

It is a massive step forward in AI in the sense that it is a general algorithm for getting good at something, quickly, with no prior knowledge of human expert strategy, the only thing it needs is rules of the game.

What an amazing achievement!

In this chapter, we will learn how it works first, then dig into one implementation to understand it better.

6.1   what is a game with perfect information

In the previous section, we mentioned a game with perfect information. What does it mean?

Quote from Wikipedia:

```
1  In game theory, a sequential game has perfect information
2  if each player, when making any decision,
3  is perfectly informed of all the events that have previously occurred,
4  including the "initialization event" of the game
5  (e.g. The starting hands of each player in a card game).
```

In other words, in a perfect information game like Go, chess, or checkers, etc, a bot can figure out what a move it should make by trying them all, then checking all possible responses by the opponent, all possible moves after that, etc.

The following figure show it more clearly:

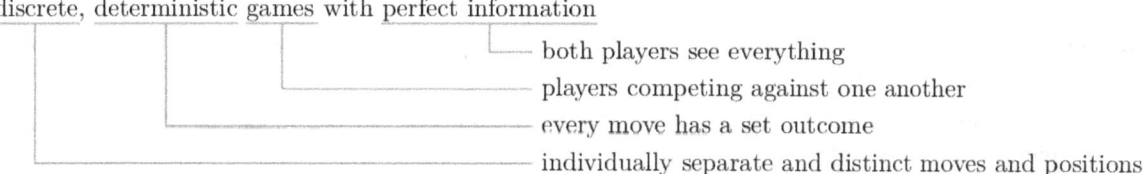

Figure 6.2: Explanation discrete,deterministic game with perfect information

If a computer was able to explore all branches for each step within reasonable playtime, no real algorithm was needed.

But for a game like Go, the number of moves/branches to try grows really fast. A rough estimation of number of legal positions on a 19x19=361 Go board could be a simple permutation of 361 moves or 361! = 10^768.

Even with current computing power, it is still impractical to explore all the possible actions within reasonable time especially at beginning or middle of the game.

Thus, generally, a computer needs a smart way, other than the brutal-force, like AlphaZero, to figure out how to play in a game.

6.2 How AlphaZero works?

The algorithm is very elegant. It is essentially like how we play a game.

When we play a bad move, it's either because we misjudged the future value of resulting positions, or we miscalculated the likelihood that our opponent would play a certain move, thus, we didn't think to explore that possibility.

Before we decide the next move of the game, we normally play through possible future scenarios mentally: we give priority to promising paths, whilst also consider how the opponent is most likely to react to our actions, then we continue to explore the unknown paths.

After reaching a certain state (some steps like deep first search or breadth-first search) that is unfamiliar, we evaluate how favorable we believe the position to be, then cascade the score back through previous positions in the mental pathway.

After we've finished exploring about future possibilities, we take an action that we think is best in its current state.

At the end of the game, we normally go back and evaluate where we misjudged the value of the future positions and update our understanding accordingly.

These are exactly two aspects of game play that AlphaZero is trained to learn.

At very high level, AlphaGo Zero and AlphaZero use **Monte Carlo Tree Search (MCST)** and DNN to simulate the self-play. With the MCST process exploring/evaluating the future paths/possibilities, DNN learning the strategies iteratively, the whole system can simulate our thought process on how to play a game and learn from previous failures.

MCTS is mainly used to gather self-play training data. It is the go-to algorithm for writing bots to play discrete, deterministic games with perfect information.

Guided by deep neural network policy, AlphaZero uses MCTS to explore some certain branches at certain depth instead of exploring all the branches.

In short: AlphaZero = MCTS + deep learning

That is basically how AlphaZero works.

Readers should be quite familiar with DNN now, so the missing piece is MCTS.

I will try to explain how MCTS works in the next section.

The following are some excellent references and documents. I strongly recommend readers to take a look.

The original paper (AlphaGo Zero) can be accessed at:
https://www.nature.com/articles/nature24270.epdf

AlphaZero could be read at:

https://arxiv.org/abs/1712.01815

http://science.sciencemag.org/content/362/6419/1140/tab-pdf

Other excellent articles:

http://web.stanford.edu/~surag/posts/alphazero.html

http://tim.hibal.org/blog/alpha-zero-how-and-why-it-works/

6.3 How MCTS works?

The following content showed several key concepts to understand MCTS.

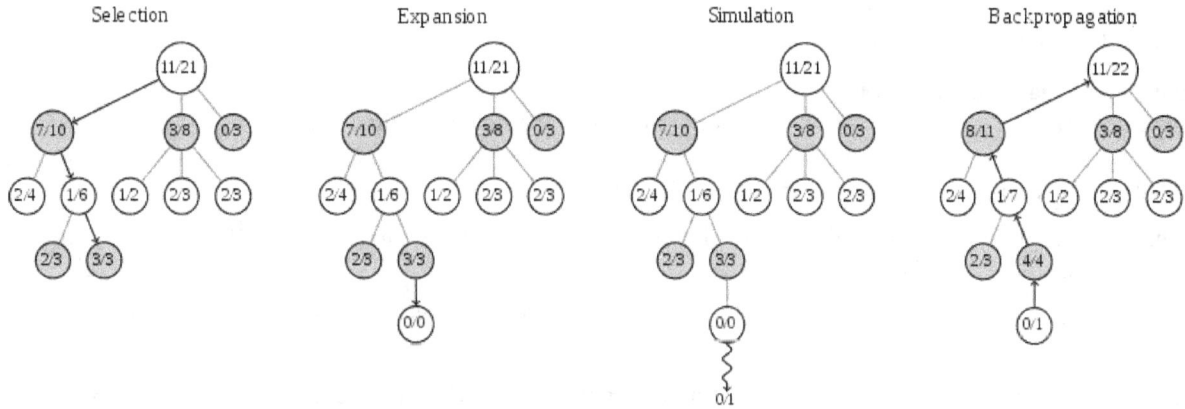

Figure 6.3: mcts tree

A game could be seen as **game tree** as above.

Each node stands for a certain **game state** s, e.g.: for a go game, it means a certain distribution of black/white stones on the go chessboard.

At a node state s, there could be several valid actions [a] that player can choose, that is called **branching factor**.

When a player chooses an action a, it will go to one of its child nodes, enter a new state.

- **visited node**: initially every node is un-visited.
  We have not evaluated this node. What does it mean? If we played an MCTS simulation starting from this node

at least once, at the end of simulation, we somehow know if we will win or lose. Thus, we backpropagate some score/reward back to that node. At that time, we call/mark that node a visited node.

- **(((simulation))**: complete one random playout from a node. This step is sometimes also called playout or rollout. A playout may be as simple as choosing uniform random moves until the game is decided (for example in chess, the game is won, lost, or drawn).

- **fully expanded node**: all of its child nodes are visited nodes.

- **backpropagation**: The simulation result is carried up from a leaf node (where simulation started) all the way back to the root node, for every node on the backpropagation path, certain statistics are computed/updated.

- **nodes' statistics**: in MCTS, we normally update

  - **total simulation reward $Q(v)$**

  - and **$N(v)$**: how many times a node has been on the backpropagation path.

- **UCT**: **Upper Confidence Bound** +, It is defined as:
  $Q(v)/N(v) + c \ sqrt\_root(log(N(v))/N(vi))$,
  where $N(v) = sum(N(vi))$ parents visited number

- **how to terminate simulation/playout**
  The game can be terminate/ended by its rule or running out of the simulation time limit we set.

With all those concepts in place, we can see how MCTS works:

Initially, the game is in an initial state s0, all its children have NOT been visited, so it is a non-fully expanded node, we need to and will visit all the children nodes.

That means for each children node, we will do the simulation, get the evaluated stats for each child's nodes, then backpropagate value to root node.

Once we finish that, we will **choose the next action by picking up a children node that maxes the UCT score as the next step** in the game.

Now, we go to this child node, and this node becomes a starting node again.

We do a similar step as before:
first, we check if it is a non-fully expanded node or not. If it is a fully expanded node that means all its child nodes (thus grandchild node from the first node point of view) have been visited/evaluated, we then use UCT to choose the next action. Otherwise, we do as previous one, visit and evaluate those un-visited node, and backpropagate value all the way up to the previous root node.

The simulation/playout will be terminated according to the termination rule we set in the game.

In short, the whole MCTS algorithm (one iteration/one round of MCTS) could be summarized as selection, expansion, simulation backpropagation.

For each round of MCTS:

- selection: start from root, and select a optimal child node base on UCT score (remember the simulation result backpropagate statistics to its root, essentially it will give some hints which node worth to continue to explore, thus prune the tree), until a leaf node node is reached. The leaf node (non fully expanded node) is a node whose children node has not been visited.

Tip

sounds recursive? The simulation give a rough estimation to prune some obviously non-optimal path, then we use that info to explore the tree further in a more refined way.

- expansion: choose one of un-visited child node. (some people say this way : create one(or more) child nodes and pick a node from one of them).

- simulation: do the simulation/rollout from that node, until game is decided (either won , lose or drawn)

- backprogration: Use the result of this playout to update node info/statics all the way back to root node.

Normally, we need to repeat multiple times/rounds of MCTS. By doing so, we want to find a way of biasing choice of child nodes that lets the game tree expand towards the most promising moves. Remember we do not want to do the brutal-force search.

In alphazero, there are some minor modifications of MCTS. For example, there is no real playout/rollout simulation (e.g: play random until the game terminated/ended) to get reward, count etc, instead, it just directly uses a policy DNN to directly predict the result from a node. See the code analysis later. Also the UCB function is a little bit different from one used in a regular MCTS. Those details could be found at reference papers before.

Some other excellent documents could be found at:

https://www.youtube.com/watch?v=UXW2yZndl7U
https://int8.io/monte-carlo-tree-seharch-beginners-guide/
http://mcts.ai/about/index.html https://towardsdatascience.com/monte-carlo-tree-search-in-reinforcement-learning

---

Tip

MCTS can also be used for non-game applications like security, physics simulation, scheduling tasks, Random walk, sample based planning etc.

6.4   alpha-zero-general - an simplified implementation analysis

So far we have a high-level view on how AlphaZero works, we need to dig into the source code to really grasp it.

An excellent python implementation can be found at:
https://github.com/suragnair/alpha-zero-general

It is a simplified, highly flexible, commented and easy to understand the implementation of self-play based reinforcement learning based on the AlphaGo Zero paper.

The framework defined a game interface so that people can easily add other games.

In the next few sections, we will try to understand this implementation.

We will choose TicTacToeGame as an example, as it is easier to understand, and take relatively short CPU time to train. For example, the training could be finished within as little as 1-2 hours on my laptop.

Since I simply do not want to copy/paste the online material here, please read the following document before proceeding:
http://web.stanford.edu/~surag/posts/alphazero.html

It should give you at least enough theoretical backgrounds to understand AlphaZero.

Even with the above reading, based on my previous experience, you may still have many questions. That is why I wrote the following code analysis to further help you to understand AlphaZero precisely by reading the code.

6.4.1   main upper level code analysis

Let's start from the very top level: main.py

By default, if you run python main.py, the game played will be Othello.

To run TicTacToeGame, we need to modify the main.py by changing one line around line 24 from g = Game(6) to g = TicTacToeGame().

Instead of ruining the main.py, I copy it as pytorch-tictactoe-main.py with that change.

To make it easy to test and follow, I forked a branch at:
https://github.com/mingewang/alpha-zero-general/tree/comrite_deep_learning

Here is the code:

```python
# pytorch-tictactoe-main.py

from Coach import Coach
from tictactoe.TicTacToeGame import TicTacToeGame
from tictactoe.pytorch.NNet import NNetWrapper as nn
from utils import *

args = dotdict({
    'numIters': 3,
    'numEps': 25,
    'tempThreshold': 15,
    'updateThreshold': 0.6,
    'maxlenOfQueue': 200000,
    'numMCTSSims': 25,
    'arenaCompare': 40,
    'cpuct': 1,

    'checkpoint': './temp/',
    'load_model': False,
    'load_folder_file': ('/dev/models/8x100x50','best.pth.tar'),
    'numItersForTrainExamplesHistory': 20,

})

if __name__=="__main__":
    g = TicTacToeGame()
    nnet = nn(g)

    if args.load_model:
        nnet.load_checkpoint(args.load_folder_file[0], args.load_folder_file[1])

    c = Coach(g, nnet, args)
    if args.load_model:
        print("Load trainExamples from file")
        c.loadTrainExamples()
    c.learn()
```

The main code should be quite easy to understand,

- Line 26, just load the game

- Line 27, create our neural network model

- Line 30, load our pre-trained data for this model if any

- Line 32, is really how to learn.

- Line 8, give us some training parameters for this framework.

Those following parameters need some attention:

- **numItes**: for each iteration (total of numItes), we play numEps times of self-plays to get the training data. Once we have training data, we train our model using a neural network. Then we pit this model against our previous model (arenaCompare times). If the new model's win rate is above updateThreshold (0.6), we will switch the model for the next iteration, otherwise, we still use the old model for the next iteration.

- **numEps**: the number of times to self-play to get training samples/data. That is something like: (s, pi, v), where s is the game state, pi is a vector of p(s,a), where a are the valid actions from s, v is the reward value on this state s. Note (s,pi,v) are vectors that record history for one self-play game from beginning to end. Actually, the DNN was trained to output (pi,v) with input s. The pi is called the **policy output**, the v represents estimated value for this state s (thinking +1 if the player wins, -1 if the player loses).

- **numMCTSSims**: inside each self-play (one of numEps), for each step (s), we need an estimation of how to get the next step. MCTS simulation can give us such information. So in a certain state s, we run numMCTSSims times of simulation to get the estimation on how to proceed from this state s. Inside this framework, it is called (MCTS.getActionProb). We will see this shortly. The return of that function is: the probability of different actions at that state s. e.g: p(s,a). The whole purpose of the simulation is to get this.

- **tempThreshold**: in each numEps self-play, before this threshold, we sort of use random action to explore possibilities, but that random is following the probability distribution given by MCTS.getActionProb. After that, we use the best action predicted from NN (MCTS.getActionProb).

Tip

what does np.random.choice(len(pi), p=pi) mean?

It generates a random sample from a given 1-D array, in this case, 0,1,2, .. len(pi) according to the distribution of pi.

So the high level pseudo-code looks like this:

```
1   foreach ( numItes ):
2     trainningSamples = []
3     foreach( numEps ):
4       train_sample = self-play()
5       trainningSamples.append( train_sample )
6     new_model = neural_network.traning( trainningSamples)
7     win_lost_rate = pit_against( new_model, prevs_model)
8     if( win_lost_rate > updateThreshold ):
9         model = new_model
10
11  self-play():
12    s in initial state
13    while( not end of the game )
14      step += 1
15      p(s,a) = getActionProb_by_MCTS_simulation(s);
16      if( step > tempThreshold) :
17        action = choose_best_estimation_from(p(s,a))
18      else:
19        action = choose_random_estimation_from(p(s,a))
20      s = move_to_next_state(a)
21
22
23  getActionProb_by_MCTS_simulation():
24    foreach(numMCTSSims):
25      mcts_search(s)
26    return p(s,a)
```

6.4.2 coach model code analysis

The coach model (Coach.py) showed how AlphaZero learns.

```
1   from collections import deque
2   from Arena import Arena
3   from MCTS import MCTS
4   import numpy as np
5   from pytorch_classification.utils import Bar, AverageMeter
6   import time, os, sys
7   from pickle import Pickler, Unpickler
```

```
8   from random import shuffle
9
10
11  class Coach():
12      """
13      This class executes the self-play + learning. It uses the functions defined
14      in Game and NeuralNet. args are specified in main.py.
15      """
16      def __init__(self, game, nnet, args):
17          self.game = game
18          # our model
19          self.nnet = nnet
20          # previous model, will replaced by nnet if
21          # nnet can beat pnet
22          self.pnet = self.nnet.__class__(self.game)  # the competitor network
23          self.args = args
24          self.mcts = MCTS(self.game, self.nnet, self.args)
25          self.trainExamplesHistory = []     # history of examples from args. ↩
                  numItersForTrainExamplesHistory latest iterations
26          self.skipFirstSelfPlay = False # can be overriden in loadTrainExamples()
27
28      def executeEpisode(self):
29          """
30          This function executes one episode of self-play, starting with player 1.
31          As the game is played, each turn is added as a training example to
32          trainExamples. The game is played till the game ends. After the game
33          ends, the outcome of the game is used to assign values to each example
34          in trainExamples.
35
36          It uses a temp=1 if episodeStep < tempThreshold, and thereafter
37          uses temp=0.
38
39          Returns:
40              trainExamples: a list of examples of the form (canonicalBoard,pi,v)
41                             pi is the MCTS informed policy vector, v is +1 if
42                             the player eventually won the game, else -1.
43          """
44          trainExamples = []
45          board = self.game.getInitBoard()
46          self.curPlayer = 1
47          episodeStep = 0
48
```

```
49      while True:
50          episodeStep += 1
51          canonicalBoard = self.game.getCanonicalForm(board,self.curPlayer)
52          # we start to choose a random action from distribution given by NN
53          # later, we choose the best action predicted by the NN
54          temp = int(episodeStep < self.args.tempThreshold)
55
56          pi = self.mcts.getActionProb(canonicalBoard, temp=temp)
57          sym = self.game.getSymmetries(canonicalBoard, pi)
58          for b,p in sym:
59              trainExamples.append([b, self.curPlayer, p, None])
60
61          # based on temp, temp=0, pi only have 1 (best) item
62          # otherwise we have a serveral items p(s,a)
63          # where a means one of the valid actions we can take
64          action = np.random.choice(len(pi), p=pi)
65          board, self.curPlayer = self.game.getNextState(board, self.curPlayer, ↩
                  action)
66
67          """
68          here we play to the end of the game!
69          think of a game of go, it could take a long long time.
70          so actually in this software
71          the game end is not really game's end
72          it is depends on our setting
73          (1) native end, mean before the upper limit steps,
74          we  know the who is winner or loser by the rule of the game
75          (2) it could be small non-zero (for draw) if we hit our upper
76          limit steps of the self-play (like 1e-4)
77          """
78          r = self.game.getGameEnded(board, self.curPlayer)
79
80          if r!=0:
81              """
82              training sample (canonicalBoard,pi,v)
83              v is the reward?
84              what is (-1)**( x[1]!=self.curPlayer )
85              """
86              return [(x[0],x[2],r*((-1)**(x[1]!=self.curPlayer))) for x in ↩
                      trainExamples]
87
88  def learn(self):
```

```
89          """
90          Performs numIters iterations with numEps episodes of self-play in each
91          iteration. After every iteration, it retrains neural network with
92          examples in trainExamples (which has a maximum length of maxlenofQueue).
93          It then pits the new neural network against the old one and accepts it
94          only if it wins >= updateThreshold fraction of games.
95          """
96
97          for i in range(1, self.args.numIters+1):
98              # bookkeeping
99              print('------ITER ' + str(i) + '------')
100             # examples of the iteration
101             if not self.skipFirstSelfPlay or i>1:
102                 iterationTrainExamples = deque([], maxlen=self.args.maxlenOfQueue ←
                        )

103
104                 eps_time = AverageMeter()
105                 bar = Bar('Self Play', max=self.args.numEps)
106                 end = time.time()
107
108                 for eps in range(self.args.numEps):
109                     self.mcts = MCTS(self.game, self.nnet, self.args)   # reset ←
                            search tree
110                     # self-play one game until the game ended
111                     # remember it is our definition of game end, not real one
112                     iterationTrainExamples += self.executeEpisode()
113
114                     # bookkeeping + plot progress
115                     eps_time.update(time.time() - end)
116                     end = time.time()
117                     bar.suffix  = '({eps}/{maxeps}) Eps Time: {et:.3f}s | Total: ←
                            {total:} | ETA: {eta:}'.format(eps=eps+1, maxeps=self. ←
                            args.numEps,et=eps_time.avg,total=bar.elapsed_td, eta=bar ←
                            .eta_td)
118                     bar.next()
119                 bar.finish()
120
121                 # save the iteration examples to the history
122                 self.trainExamplesHistory.append(iterationTrainExamples)
123
124             if len(self.trainExamplesHistory) > self.args. ←
                    numItersForTrainExamplesHistory:
```

```
125     print("len(trainExamplesHistory) =", len(self. ↵
            trainExamplesHistory), " => remove the oldest trainExamples")
126     self.trainExamplesHistory.pop(0)
127 # backup history to a file
128 # NB! the examples were collected using the model from the previous ↵
        iteration, so (i-1)
129 self.saveTrainExamples(i-1)
130
131 # shuffle examlpes before training
132 trainExamples = []
133 for e in self.trainExamplesHistory:
134     trainExamples.extend(e)
135 shuffle(trainExamples)
136
137 # training new network, keeping a copy of the old one
138 self.nnet.save_checkpoint(folder=self.args.checkpoint, filename='temp ↵
        .pth.tar')
139 self.pnet.load_checkpoint(folder=self.args.checkpoint, filename='temp ↵
        .pth.tar')
140 pmcts = MCTS(self.game, self.pnet, self.args)
141
142 self.nnet.train(trainExamples)
143 nmcts = MCTS(self.game, self.nnet, self.args)
144
145 print('PITTING AGAINST PREVIOUS VERSION')
146 arena = Arena(lambda x: np.argmax(pmcts.getActionProb(x, temp=0)),
147             lambda x: np.argmax(nmcts.getActionProb(x, temp=0)), ↵
                self.game)
148
149 # self-play/competed with previous model by number of self.args. ↵
        arenaCompare games
150 pwins, nwins, draws = arena.playGames(self.args.arenaCompare)
151
152 print('NEW/PREV WINS : %d / %d ; DRAWS : %d' % (nwins, pwins, draws))
153 if pwins+nwins > 0 and float(nwins)/(pwins+nwins) < self.args. ↵
        updateThreshold:
154     print('REJECTING NEW MODEL')
155     self.nnet.load_checkpoint(folder=self.args.checkpoint, filename=' ↵
            temp.pth.tar')
156 else:
157     print('ACCEPTING NEW MODEL')
158     self.nnet.save_checkpoint(folder=self.args.checkpoint, filename= ↵
```

```
                         self.getCheckpointFile(i))
159              self.nnet.save_checkpoint(folder=self.args.checkpoint, filename=' ↵
                     best.pth.tar')
160
161     def getCheckpointFile(self, iteration):
162         return 'checkpoint_' + str(iteration) + '.pth.tar'
163
164     def saveTrainExamples(self, iteration):
165         folder = self.args.checkpoint
166         if not os.path.exists(folder):
167             os.makedirs(folder)
168         filename = os.path.join(folder, self.getCheckpointFile(iteration)+". ↵
                examples")
169         with open(filename, "wb+") as f:
170             Pickler(f).dump(self.trainExamplesHistory)
171         f.closed
172
173     def loadTrainExamples(self):
174         modelFile = os.path.join(self.args.load_folder_file[0], self.args. ↵
                load_folder_file[1])
175         examplesFile = modelFile+".examples"
176         if not os.path.isfile(examplesFile):
177             print(examplesFile)
178             r = input("File with trainExamples not found. Continue? [y|n]")
179             if r != "y":
180                 sys.exit()
181         else:
182             print("File with trainExamples found. Read it.")
183             with open(examplesFile, "rb") as f:
184                 self.trainExamplesHistory = Unpickler(f).load()
185             f.closed
186             # examples based on the model were already collected (loaded)
187             self.skipFirstSelfPlay = True
```

- Line 88 is the start of the learn() function, the basic structure is similar to what we mentioned in the main code analysis.

- Line 102 we defined a dequeue to hold our training samples.

- Line 112 is to run one self-play (executeEpisode) to get training data.

- Line 122 : just save our training data into a history buffer, so we always use the latest numItersForTrainExamplesHistory of sample to train our model

- Line 138-139, we first save our current model's data, then load it into a previous model

- Line 142, we use data to train our current model.

- Line 140, 143: prepare an MCTS search using our current and previous model for future pitting against each other.

- Line 146, set up an arena so that both models can complete again each other.

- Line 150, using arena to pit each other arenaCompare of times, and get the win-lose rate.

- Line 153-159, check the win-loss rate. If the new model is better, we just switch to use it for the next iteration.

- Line 28, really define executeEpisode(), which plays one game based on the current model. That means each player play against each other using the same policy MCTS. The return result is a list of: (s, pi, v),
  where s : stands for certain state,
  pi: is p(s,a) which is the probability to take action a at current state s
  v: current reward or value of this state s.

6.4.3   MCST code analysis

Now let's look at the code for MCTS (MCTS.py)

```
1   import math
2   import numpy as np
3   EPS = 1e-8
4
5   class MCTS():
6       """
7       This class handles the MCTS tree.
8       """
9
10      def __init__(self, game, nnet, args):
11          self.game = game
12          self.nnet = nnet
13          self.args = args
14          # the expected reward for taking action a from state s
```

```
15          # it is python set, mutable containers of items of arbitrary types, with  ←
              no duplicate
16          # with s,a as parameter
17          # e.g; self.Qsa[(s,a)] = (self.Nsa[(s,a)]*self.Qsa[(s,a)] + v)/(self.Nsa ←
              [(s,a)]+1)
18          self.Qsa = {}         # stores Q values for s,a (as defined in the paper)
19          # e.g: self.Nsa[(s,a)] += 1
20          self.Nsa = {}         # stores #times edge s,a was visited
21          # e.g: self.Ns[s] += 1
22          self.Ns = {}          # stores #times board s was visited
23          self.Ps = {}          # stores initial policy (returned by neural net)
24
25          self.Es = {}          # stores game.getGameEnded ended for board s
26          self.Vs = {}          # stores game.getValidMoves for board s
27
28      # what is the return?
29      def getActionProb(self, canonicalBoard, temp=1):
30          """
31          This function performs numMCTSSims simulations of MCTS starting from
32          canonicalBoard.
33
34          Returns:
35              probs: a policy vector where the probability of the ith action is
36                     proportional to Nsa[(s,a)]**(1./temp)
37          """
38
39          # play many times, always start from the same state
40          # so that we explore hopefully most valuable route to win
41          for i in range(self.args.numMCTSSims):
42              # search will play until leaf node was found
43              self.search(canonicalBoard)
44
45          s = self.game.stringRepresentation(canonicalBoard)
46          # if action was not in the N(s,a), that means we never chose that action
47          # thus not useable in the future
48          counts = [self.Nsa[(s,a)] if (s,a) in self.Nsa else 0 for a in range(self ←
              .game.getActionSize())]
49
50          # temperate 0 means we always choose the best route
51          if temp==0:
52              bestA = np.argmax(counts)
53              probs = [0]*len(counts)
```

```
54              probs[bestA]=1
55              return probs
56
57          # we return probably so coach/replay pit can use this to determine
58          # which action to choose
59          counts = [x**(1./temp) for x in counts]
60          probs = [x/float(sum(counts)) for x in counts]
61          return probs
62
63      # The function returns either a new leaf node is found
64      # or a terminated node is found.
65      # The end of game was defined by game, maybe not real native end of the game
66      # we then back propagate the Qsa(s,q), Nsa(s,a) etc
67      #
68      # Thus getActionProb() loop will start again from very beginning
69      # node to do the simulation again ( sort of BFS ) based on the new data
70      def search(self, canonicalBoard):
71          """
72          This function performs one iteration of MCTS. It is recursively called
73          till a leaf node is found. The action chosen at each node is one that
74          has the maximum upper confidence bound as in the paper.
75
76          Once a leaf node is found, the neural network is called to return an
77          initial policy P and a value v for the state. This value is propagated
78          up the search path. In case the leaf node is a terminal state, the
79          outcome is propagated up the search path. The values of Ns, Nsa, Qsa are
80          updated.
81
82          NOTE: the return values are the negative of the value of the current
83          state. This is done since v is in [-1,1] and if v is the value of a
84          state for the current player, then its value is -v for the other player.
85
86          Returns:
87              v: the negative of the value of the current canonicalBoard
88          """
89
90          # s is hashRepresentation from current board state
91          s = self.game.stringRepresentation(canonicalBoard)
92
93          if s not in self.Es:
94              self.Es[s] = self.game.getGameEnded(canonicalBoard, 1)
95
```

```
96          if self.Es[s]!=0:
97              # terminal node, negative for the next player, as we play games
98              return -self.Es[s]
99
100         # new node
101         if s not in self.Ps:
102             # what is a leaf node? a new node?
103             # remember we recursively call ourself
104             # NN is take native state instead of s as input
105             self.Ps[s], v = self.nnet.predict(canonicalBoard)
106             # valid move from current state
107             valids = self.game.getValidMoves(canonicalBoard, 1)
108             #  a binary vector of length self.getActionSize(), 1 for
109             # moves that are valid from the current board and player,
110             # 0 for invalid moves
111             self.Ps[s] = self.Ps[s]*valids        # masking invalid movesh
112
113             sum_Ps_s = np.sum(self.Ps[s])
114             # why? since we did mask?
115             if sum_Ps_s > 0:
116                 self.Ps[s] /= sum_Ps_s     # renormalize
117             else:
118                 # if all valid moves were masked make all valid moves equally  ←
                        probable

120                 # NB! All valid moves may be masked if either your NNet  ←
                        architecture is insufficient or you've got overfitting or  ←
                        something else.
121                 # If you have got dozens or hundreds of these messages you should ←
                        pay attention to your NNet and/or training process.
122                 print("All valid moves were masked, do workaround.")
123                 self.Ps[s] = self.Ps[s] + valids
124                 self.Ps[s] /= np.sum(self.Ps[s])
125
126             self.Vs[s] = valids
127             self.Ns[s] = 0
128             return -v
129
130         valids = self.Vs[s]
131         cur_best = -float('inf')
132         best_act = -1
133
```

```
134        # pick the action with the highest upper confidence bound
135        # among valid move
136        for a in range(self.game.getActionSize()):
137            if valids[a]:
138                if (s,a) in self.Qsa:
139                    u = self.Qsa[(s,a)] + self.args.cpuct*self.Ps[s][a]*math.sqrt ↵
                           (self.Ns[s])/(1+self.Nsa[(s,a)])
140                else:
141                    u = self.args.cpuct*self.Ps[s][a]*math.sqrt(self.Ns[s] + EPS) ↵
                           # Q = 0 ?
142
143                if u > cur_best:
144                    cur_best = u
145                    best_act = a
146
147        # got best estimated action
148        a = best_act
149        # what is next_s?
150        next_s, next_player = self.game.getNextState(canonicalBoard, 1, a)
151        # why need this? is not next_s a state from current player or next_player ↵
               ?
152        # always from certain point of view from certain player
153        # the canonical form can be chosen to be from the pov
154        # returns canonical form of board. The canonical form
155        # should be independent of player. For e.g. in chess,
156        # of white. When the player is white, we can return
157        # board as is. When the player is black, we can invert
158        # the colors and return the board?
159        next_s = self.game.getCanonicalForm(next_s, next_player)
160
161        # return reward from next player's view
162        v = self.search(next_s)
163
164        # at the end of search, we update
165        if (s,a) in self.Qsa:
166            # this is an avg reward
167            self.Qsa[(s,a)] = (self.Nsa[(s,a)]*self.Qsa[(s,a)] + v)/(self.Nsa[(s, ↵
                   a)]+1)
168            self.Nsa[(s,a)] += 1
169
170        else:
171            self.Qsa[(s,a)] = v
```

```
172          self.Nsa[(s,a)] = 1
173
174        self.Ns[s] += 1
175        return -v
```

- Line 29 defines that getActionProb which was used in the coach module. It does the simulation several times to get the estimation status of this node/state.

- Line 41-43, we simulation numMCTSSims times of MCTS search. At each search/play, we will stop at either a new leaf node or termination node was found, and update node information/statistics, this will cause UCB score changes for the next round of MCTS. Then we start another round of MCTS from this state/node again based on new information/statistics.

- Line 48, we filter out non-valid action.

- Line 51-61, depending on the temp (either 0 or 1), we return the estimated probability distribution on this state p(s,a).
  Essentially, after numMCTSSims times of MCTS, we get a good sense/picture of what those nodes/score looks like, sod that we know how to win based on those info.

- Line 70 defined the core part of **one round of MCTS search**.

- Line 93 - 98, just check if the game is ended or not. If it ends, we return.

- Line 101-128, we found a new leaf node never visited before. According to MCTS regular framework, we should do the **simulation**. The normal simulation means: we should have a while loop to play out from current state canonicalBoard, until we can decide who win. But here, we just used the DNN to predict the win/lose result directly as v is the result of the DNN's prediction instead of doing the real simulation.

- Line 136-145, we meet a node which has been visited/estimated before, now based on the previous estimation, we use UCT to choose the best next action a. According to MCTS regular framework, this step is the **selection**.

- Line 150, we use that action a to play the game to the next state. According to MCTS regular framework, this step is the **expansion**.

- Line 162, now reach the next_s state, we play recursively using this function to get the estimated value of next_s. It will return if it found a new leaf node or the game is terminated. According to MCTS regular framework, this step is the **simulation**. The author wrote this function as a recursive function, so we do the simulation as shown in Line 101-128.

- Line 165-175, we update our node's stats. The recursive function will actually backpropagate those stats all the way back to the root node we started. According to MCTS regular framework, this step is the **backprogation**.

6.4.4   other source codes, models

I tried to explain the main core/key part of alpha-zero-general. Other parts hopefully should be relatively easy to follow and understand.

Even with those explanations, code analysis, to fully understand AlphaZero, my guess is you may need to read those source code analysis, previous documents and references back and forth several times, just as I did.

It is quite a complicated system, so it takes time to digest.

6.4.5   how to train the game

Here is how to train the game:

python3 pytorch-tictactoe-main.py

```
1   (pytorch_env)$ python pytorch-tictactoe-main.py
2   ------ITER 1------
3   Self Play |##                              | (2/25) Eps Time: 4.717s | Total:  ←
        0:00:09 | ETA: 0:01:46
4   Self Play |############################|  (25/25) Eps Time: 5.645s | Total:  ←
        0:02:21 | ETA: 0:00:06
5   Checkpoint Directory exists!
6   EPOCH ::: 1
7   Training Net |#    | (1/21) Data: 0.001s | Batch: 8.402s | Total: 0:00:08 | ETA:  ←
        0:00:00 | Loss_pi: 2.3815 | Loss_v:
8   Training Net |###    | (2/21) Data: 0.001s | Batch: 8.422s | Total: 0:00:16 | ETA  ←
        : 0:02:49 | Loss_pi: 2.3432 | Loss_v:
9   ...
10
11  EPOCH ::: 2 0.583
12  PITTING AGAINST PREVIOUS VERSION
13  Arena.playGames |############################|  (41/20) Eps Time: 3.012s |  ←
        Total: 0:02:00 | ETA: 0:00:02
14  NEW/PREV WINS : 15 / 13 ; DRAWS : 12
15  REJECTING NEW MODEL
16  ------ITER 2------
17  ...
18  ...
19
20  PITTING AGAINST PREVIOUS VERSION
```

```
21  Arena.playGames |################################| (41/20) Eps Time: 2.291s |  ↩
        Total: 0:01:31 | ETA: 0:00:02
22  NEW/PREV WINS : 12 / 0 ; DRAWS : 28
23  ACCEPTING NEW MODEL
24  Checkpoint Directory exists!
25  Checkpoint Directory exists!
```

Depending on your computer, it may take up to 1 hr to train.

The saved model is at: temp/best.pth.tar, we can copy it to:

```
1  mkdir -p pretrained_models/tictactoe/pytorch/
2  cp temp/best.pth.tar pretrained_models/tictactoe/pytorch/best-25eps-25sim-10epch. ↩
        pth.tar
```

6.4.6   how to play the game

Now the fun part, let's play with trained model:

python pytorch-tictactoe-pit.py

Tip
You input (x,y) to tell which position you want to play, the computer will show you available (x,y) you can input.

```
1  (pytorch_env) $ python ./pytorch-tictactoe-pit.py
2  Turn  1 Player  1
3     0 1 2
4     --------
5  0 |- - - |
6  1 |- - - |
7  2 |- - - |
8     --------
9  Turn  2 Player  -1
10    0 1 2
11    --------
12 0 |- - - |
```

```
13    1 |- O - |
14    2 |- - - |
15      --------
16    0 0
17    0 1
18    0 2
19    1 0
20    1 2
21    2 0
22    2 1
23    2 2
24    0 0
25    Turn  3 Player  1
26       0 1 2
27      --------
28    0 |X - - |
29    1 |- O - |
30    2 |- - - |
31      --------
32    Turn  4 Player  -1
33       0 1 2
34      --------
35    0 |X O - |
36    1 |- O - |
37    2 |- - - |
38      --------
39    0 2
40    1 0
41    1 2
42    2 0
43    2 1
44    2 2
45    2 1
46    Turn  5 Player  1
47       0 1 2
48      --------
49    0 |X O - |
50    1 |- O - |
51    2 |- X - |
52      --------
53    Turn  6 Player  -1
54       0 1 2
```

```
55    --------
56  0 |X O - |
57  1 |- O - |
58  2 |O X - |
59    --------
60  0 2
61  1 0
62  1 2
63  2 2
```

Is it not that fun!

6.5   applications of AlphaAero

AlphaZero shines in the area of computer games with perfect information, but remember it is a generic reinforcement learning algorithm, so it could probably be applied to many other RL areas as well.

Use your imagination!

6.6   summary

In this chapter, we learned the amazing break-through AlphaZero technology. In particular, you should:

- understand how AlphaZero works generally

- understand MCST

- be able to adopt alpha-zero-general to other games (for advanced readers).

Chapter 7

Index

About the author

Benjamin Young is the owner of www.comrite.com, an information technology consulting firm based in Austin, TX, specialized in software development (machine/deep learning, voip, web development etc). He has more than 20 years experience in software engineering, system/network administration.

He can be reached at: benjamin@comrite.com

Or by visiting:

http://amazon.com/author/benjaminyoung

https://github.com/mingewang/

AND PLEASE ...

If you find this book useful, I'd really appreciate a review (no matter how short) on amazon:

Vol. 1: https://www.amazon.com/gp/product/B08JKQLB8Z

Vol. 2: https://www.amazon.com/gp/product/B08JKPS7N5

This will help me continue to write quality books.

Other books by Benjamin Young:

- Deep Learning with Keras from Scratch:
  https://www.amazon.com/gp/product/1091838828/

- Docker for Dummies in Real World:
  https://www.amazon.com/dp/B06Y295S49/

- Kubernetes Quick Start:
  https://www.amazon.com/dp/B08HQTM57N/